Normal Eating® for Normal Weight

The Path to Freedom from Weight Obsession and Food Cravings

Sheryl Canter, M.A.

Permutations Software, Inc.

Sheryl Canter
Permutations Software, Inc.
302A W 12th St, #267
New York, NY 10014
USA

sheryl@normaleating.com
http://normaleating.com

"Normal Eating" is a registered trademark of Permutations Software, Inc.

Library of Congress Control Number: 2009901713

ISBN-10: 0-9630781-7-8
ISBN-13: 978-0-9630781-7-9

Note: This book is sold with the understanding that the publisher is not engaged in rendering psychological, medical, or other professional services. The publisher and the author disclaim any liability in connection with the use of information herein. Readers are encouraged to adapt the book's suggestions and advice to suit their own needs and limitations. Names and other identifying information of clients discussed in this book have been changed or removed to protect their privacy.

Visit NormalEating.com to join our online Support Group.

This book is dedicated to the memory of my mother, Lenore Engel Canter, who believed in this project and believed in me.

CONTENTS

WHY DIETING DOESN'T WORK

COMPULSIVE EATING & SELF-LOVE

Contents

The Normal Eating Method

Issues & Answers

Acknowledgments

Many people made this book possible. I'm especially grateful to my brother, Neil Canter, for his unfailing support and eagle-eyed proofreading, and my talented sister, Nina Fresco, who designed the cover and instructed me in the use of fonts and design software.

I'm also grateful to the brave and loving members of the Normal Eating Support Group, on the Web at NormalEating.com, whose questions and feedback made this a better book.

INTRODUCTION
SHERYL'S STORY

I was introduced to the idea that dieting was dangerous, self-negating, and unnecessary back in 1978, when Susie Orbach published her landmark book *Fat is a Feminist Issue*. Like many young women, I had been on the diet-binge-self-loathing merry-go-round since Junior High School. This book put a stop to it. The ideas Orbach put forth had never occurred to me, and I knew she was right.

I still have my original copy of *Fat is a Feminist Issue*. The pages are brown with age, and covered with underlining and penciled notes. I followed every suggestion and tried every exercise, even recording the guided fantasies on cassette tapes so I could do them. And of course, I stopped dieting. I lost 30 pounds without trying, and was slim for the first time since puberty.

At this time I was working on a Master's degree in Counseling at New York University, and doing a practicum at the New York University Counseling Center. I started a group for women with compulsive eating problems based on the ideas in *Fat is a Feminist Issue*. The group was extremely popular, and also effective. Participants stopped dieting and explored the issues that triggered their eating, and everybody's weight moved towards normal. (This meant weight loss for all but one member who struggled with anorexia.) Even more important was the feeling of empowerment and validation from throwing off the bonds of dieting.

But although this marked the end dieting for me, it wasn't the end of my struggle with weight. Being a normal weight caused some unanticipated problems. I was uncomfortable with the change in how men responded to me. I also continued to use food as a way to cope during times of stress, so my weight would periodically shoot up again. When the stressful situation resolved, my weight would drop back down without my even thinking about it. I'd notice my clothes were getting big, I'd get on the scale, and discover I'd lost 20 pounds — at which point I often started gaining again because this made me anxious.

My periods of normal eating prevented continuous weight gain over time, which I'm sure is what would have happened if I'd continued dieting. I know I'd have ended up much more than 30 pounds overweight since I never would have lost what I gained during times of stress. This up-and-down pattern wasn't completely satisfactory, but it was much better than what I was doing before. I didn't worry too much about the periodic weight gains because I always eventually lost it again. 75% recovery was good enough for a long time.

Then in 2000 – more than 20 years after I'd stopped dieting, I was faced with a problem that required more than 75% recovery. My ulcerative colitis, which had been mostly in remission, began to flare badly. Medication was not controlling it, so I researched alternative treatments on the internet. What I found was the last thing in the world someone with my background would want to find: Eliminating grain and dairy can resolve autoimmune problems such as ulcerative colitis for some people.

I didn't take this well, and in fact I refused to even try the diet for nearly a year. But I kept getting sicker and sicker, and eventually I got desperate. I tried it for three months and it worked – the colitis went into remission. And I went straight back into the diet crazies. I started overeating the foods I was allowed to eat, and my weight began to climb.

Feeling desperate, I did something that, in retrospect, seems amazing given my previous experience. I tried to lose weight by dieting – counting calories and carbs. Apparently I'd been away from Susie Orbach's book for too long.

Naturally I couldn't stick to this and gained even more weight, so then I tried Overeater's Anonymous. They said my problem was a physical addiction to sugar, so I gave up all refined sugar for six months. That didn't work, either. I just overate other foods.

Then finally (I don't know why it took me so long), I remembered what worked for me back in 1978. One day after an OA meeting, I talked to someone about my experience with attuned eating and how I wished I could get back to that. She told me about Geneen Roth, whose first books were published in the early 1980's. I hadn't read any books on attuned eating since *Fat is a Feminist Issue*, so this was new to me.

I loved Geneen Roth's books because they showed me how to have compassion for myself. But they didn't focus enough on method. I liked what she was saying, but I couldn't see how to get there, even though I'd been there before. Attuned eating didn't come as easily to me the second time around.

I thought a support group might help, so I looked online and found a group based on the book *Overcoming Overeating* by Hirschmann and Munter. I gained another 10 pounds following their bad advice (for more on this, see the section on "Overcoming Overeating"), and it seemed like everyone else on the list was gaining, too. I posted a message saying the advice didn't feel right and asking if anyone on the list had lost weight. The moderator sent me private email saying that I was disrupting the group and unsubscribed me.

INTRODUCTION

So I started my own online group called Normal Eating.
The first time I stopped dieting, I lost the obsession and
excess weight quickly and easily. But this time I struggled. I
realize now it was because I was so anxious about whether
I would lose the weight. I kept turning attuned eating into
the "eat when hungry diet". Finally I got so sick of the whole
thing that I decided I didn't care what I weighed. And that
is when I finally lost the weight. I realized that this was the
missing key: desperation to lose weight prevents you from
eating normally and losing weight.

This insight is where Normal Eating departs from other
attuned eating approaches: An excessive concern with how
much you weigh is identified as itself a problem. This is
not a fat acceptance philosophy; it's a crucial observation
about what prevents people from eating according to body
wisdom. If you are terrified of gaining weight or desperate
to lose it, you cannot hear the whisper of body wisdom and
eat in accordance with it.

The stages and exercises that make up Normal Eating were
born of my personal struggle as well as my professional
training, and improved by feedback from Normal Eating
Support Group members. The questions they asked showed
me where I needed to clarify and expand. The result is a
very practical manual for solving the problem of compulsive eating: Normal Eating for Normal Weight.

WHO THIS BOOK CAN HELP

Your history doesn't have to be exactly like mine to benefit from Normal Eating. The response from Normal Eating Support Group members has been overwhelmingly positive, and they are a diverse group. They vary from severely underweight (anorexic) to severely overweight. Some have never been more than 10-20 pounds overweight, but are sick of being obsessed with eating and body size. Some joined after losing 100+ pounds because they were still obsessed; they know better than anyone that weight is a side issue. Some have a history of chronic dieting, some don't. Some have a history of binge eating, while others graze all day. Some have struggled with bulimia, while others have not.

But they were all helped by Normal Eating. What they have in common is a history of eating for emotional reasons, and that is what Normal Eating addresses. Support Group members say that Normal Eating has helped them as nothing before has.

The Normal Eating Support Group is an effective adjunct to the book, providing a place to ask questions and get support as you work through your issues. To join, please visit NormalEating.com.

PART 1
WHY DIETING
DOESN'T WORK

DESPERATELY SEEKING SLIMNESS

Being fat is not the problem; it's a symptom of the problem. That's why diets don't lead to permanent weight loss. You might lose weight initially, but the internal conflicts that caused the weight gain remain so eventually you gain it back. Diets are the tail wagging the dog – changing your outside without changing your inside.

Normal Eating is a step-by-step guide to fixing the real problem, the underlying triggers. As you free yourself from food and weight obsession and learn true self-care, normal weight follows naturally as a side effect. You lose weight without dieting, and without obsessing on every mouthful you eat.

Ironically, when weight loss is the direct goal, it becomes virtually unattainable because a focus on weight loss prevents you from eating normally. To become your normal weight, your goal must be to stop obsessing about your food intake and body size. Then you will be able to reconnect with body wisdom, eat normally, and return naturally to your normal weight.

THE CRUCIAL SHIFT IN ATTITUDE

This shift in focus away from your weight is crucial. But it doesn't mean not caring about your weight at all. It's natural to feel sad or disappointed about being fat, or to feel a sense of loss if you once were slim. But feeling desperation and despair about your weight is an overreaction unless your weight has become a health issue. Even then, there is a tendency to overemphasize the importance of weight and underemphasize what really matters.

In the scheme of things, being a good person, fulfilling your responsibilities, loving your family and friends, and making good use of the talents and gifts you've been given are far more important than how much you weigh! Perhaps you'd prefer to be slim, but it shouldn't be a key determinant of your sense of value or self-worth. Wanting to be slim is normal; dying to be slim – feeling absolutely desperate to be slim – is not normal.

How do you stop caring so much about how much you weigh? Pretending you don't care won't work. But as you read this book and do the exercises, you'll learn to put your weight in perspective.

For many people, the turning point is when they finally get angry — not at themselves, but at the culture and diet industry that has caused them so much pain. When they get sick of the whole diet merry-go-round and decide they'd rather be at peace than be slim, they finally start to lose weight. It's a classic Zen paradox. Wanting it pushes it farther away.

BODY SIZE OBSESSION

Sometimes insight is a simple matter of reversing cause and effect. Your body size isn't the cause of your weight obsession; your weight obsession is the cause of your body size. One of the most frequently expressed disappointments of people who have lost weight through dieting is that the obsession did not go away — it was independent of what they weighed.

So why the obsession? There are many reasons, not the least of which is our weight-obsessed culture (more on this later). But emotional eating and weight obsession often begin with a life problem that's even more disturbing than being fat. Usually it's something we feel powerless over, like health problems, financial problems, or difficulties with a loved one.

Compulsive eating and being fat are sufficiently painful to be an effective distraction, while at the same time provoking less anxiety than the real problem because they are potentially under our control. We can always resolve to go on a diet, but what are we going to do about a bad marriage or a sick child?

The obsession with weight loss often grows into a magical belief that life would be wonderful if only we were slim. But being slim doesn't guarantee happiness. There are many normal weight people in this world who are unhappy. Still, people like to think they'd be happy if only they lost weight, because then happiness seems in reach with the next diet or weight loss scheme. If we allowed our real problems into awareness, it might feel like we never could be happy.

The fantasy bursts with weight loss. Many people who have lost weight feel great anxiety when being slim doesn't lead to the happiness they imagined it would. The anxiety comes from the fear that happiness isn't possible. That's not true, of course. They just haven't dealt with the real problems, and may have great fear in doing so. Sometimes people regain the weight they've lost so they can regain the fantasy that they just need to lose weight and all will be well. Seems strange, but it's true.

A CULTURAL OBSESSION

An obsession with slimness is not something we invented ourselves out of whole cloth. It's a cultural myth that slenderness brings happiness, communicated in dozens of ways, everywhere we turn. You can't look at a magazine or television program without being inundated with weight loss tips and smiling underweight models.

We live in a weight-obsessed culture. The obsession is like a contagious disease that we all catch shortly after birth. When girls start to menstruate, bone density increases dramatically, precipitating a weight gain of 10-15 pounds. Sadly, teenage girls often misinterpret this weight gain as "getting fat". They respond by dieting, and the pattern of disordered eating begins.

Beauty: Inner & Outer

Our culture equates physical beauty with value as a human being. This overemphasis on physical beauty, not surprisingly, instills a desperate need to be beautiful. Worse, our culture has, for some reason, come up with a standard of beauty for women that requires being underweight. Most women cannot look the way society says they should look by eating normally – that is, eating according to hunger and satiation cues. The only way to achieve society's standard of beauty is through an unnatural diet that leaves you hungry all the time.

Many actresses, dancers, models, and other women who make a living with their looks maintain a weight that is below what's normal for them. At best this means living with being hungry all the time. Newswoman Diane Sawyer has talked about this, and so has former model Tyra Banks. But many models and dancers have serious eating disorders like anorexia or bulimia.

SHIFTING STANDARDS OF BEAUTY

Gauntness is not a universal characteristic of female beauty. Throughout human history until the 1920s, the ideal for feminine beauty was full breasts, wide hips, and rounded tummies – just look at Renoir and other artists from earlier times. Sexy women were voluptuous and curvy. To be too skinny was considered unfeminine. Even today, thinness is associated with harshness, poverty, and meanness in many non-Western cultures, for example in certain parts of Africa.

The adolescent boy look (no hips and no breasts) first became an ideal in the 1920s with flappers and the women's suffrage movement. It is thought by some cultural anthropologists to be an outgrowth of resentment towards women's independence. Essentially women were being told that if they wanted independence, they needed to look more like men. But the cross-cultural, cross-time feminine ideal is to be curved and soft, not angular.

Nor is it healthy for women to be excessively thin. When women's body fat drops below 14% or so, they stop menstruating. Women are not meant to be skinny. They are designed to carry extra fat as insurance for when they're pregnant. Strong, healthy, normal-weight women tend to be rounded, not angular. When we get too thin, the female parts of us cease to function!

Moreover, men are biologically programmed to prefer women who look like they'd be good at making babies – women with broad hips and large breasts, Marilyn Monroe not Twiggy. That's why (biologically speaking) thin women were considered unattractive for most of history. Extremely thin women don't menstruate and can't produce offspring at all.

What's naturally attractive is youth and health. All the classic characteristics of beauty, cross-time and cross-culture, are signs of youth and health: clear, smooth skin, shiny hair, bright eyes, firm muscle tone. But even when we are young, healthy, and beautiful, we don't know it. Most young women feel fat and ugly. They don't realize until they are middle-aged, when they look back at pictures of themselves, how beautiful they really were. If you think it's a shame that you couldn't enjoy your beauty when you had it, then consider that 20 years from now, you'll look back at pictures of yourself today and wish you'd appreciated the youth and beauty you have today.

Society's overemphasis on physical beauty is unfortunate, however, no matter what the standard. You need to be able to look in the mirror and accept what you see. How do you do that? First, by recognizing that you don't need physical perfection to be attractive. Women (and men) can be sexy and appealing without a perfect face and figure. But what's most important to realize is that inner beauty matters much more than outer beauty – even in this upside down world.

INNER BEAUTY

Have you ever met someone with the gift of being able to truly focus on others? When you talk to someone like this, you feel interesting, important, and heard. People like this attract others like magnets, no matter what they look like. The power of character can break through all the cultural silliness about physical appearance.

What makes people like this so attractive is their inner peace. A person who is peaceful and quiet within can focus on others in a genuine way that others sense and respond to. When a peaceful person meets someone new, her focus is on learning about this new person, rather than what kind of impression she is making. She has no internal anxiety competing for her attention.

When people feel insecure, they can be so absorbed with how they look and whether they are liked that it doesn't occur to them that others would appreciate a warm greeting. They don't think of themselves as having some-thing to give, and their internal discomfort is so distracting that they may hardly be aware of others' feelings.

Most of the time, these worries are baseless. A story posted by a woman in the Normal Eating Support Group illustrates this beautifully:

> A year or two ago, I was at a busy train station and a really attractive woman looked me up and down and then saw that I saw her and she looked away. About a dozen thoughts raced through my head. "She thinks I'm fat", "She thinks I'm unfashionable", "She doesn't like my face", "She can tell I'm irrational"…you get the picture.
>
> After a moment or two of watching the train arrival/ departure board she approached me and I got really nervous. I have NO idea what I thought she was going to do to me, but I had decided that I needed to protect myself. Anyway, she gets to me and said, "Excuse me, but I think your shoes are soooo cute. Do you mind if I ask you where you got them so that I can get a pair?"

By its nature, concern with one's weight and appearance is a concern with self. We enter a room and think everyone is staring at us and thinking we are fat. We scowl at people because we imagine they don't like us. Think how different our experience would be if we smiled and tried to make others feel comfortable, instead of worrying about what they thought of us.

Simply acknowledging the humans you encounter during the day, noticing that they are sensate beings with feelings, smiling at them, and showing genuine interest in them, can markedly improve the quality of your life and relationships. You will start to realize that if someone is scowling or grouchy, it may not be about you! What a concept! We are not in the center of everyone's mind!

GETTING OUT OF YOURSELF

There is an old Chinese fable about a woman who was depressed because her family was killed. She went to the village wise man for help, and he told her to collect mustard seeds from three homes that had never known sorrow. With this he could make a potion that would lift the pain in her heart.

She went from house to house asking if people had experienced sorrow. At each home she went to, she heard another heart-breaking story. She discovered that sorrow had visited every single home. Soon instead of focusing on herself and her problems, she was listening to others and trying to help them. And voilà! Her own sorrow lifted. When she was able to focus outward, her entire outlook changed.

I have to end this chapter with a warning, however. There is a difference between the loving other-focus of a person who is peaceful within, and the self-denying other-focus of codependency – taking care of others while ignoring your own needs. I'll talk more about this in the chapter on codependency.

OUR EATING-
DISORDERED CULTURE

Our modern society views enjoyment of eating in much the same way as Victorians viewed enjoyment of sex – dangerous and sinful, something to feel guilty about. It's considered almost obscene not to be on a diet that restricts what you eat. If you tell someone you've decided not to diet anymore, you risk an earful about what a dangerous mistake you're making, how natural appetites

29

have no natural limits, and the only way to have control is through dieting.

But this makes no sense! Natural limits are part of our natural instincts.

Going on your first diet is practically a rite of passage into adulthood for young women. It's considered an obvious truth that, left to our own devices, we would never stop eating. We need a diet.

This message is profoundly destructive. When we ignore our inner cues about what, when, and how much to eat, we eventually lose the ability to read these cues. When we become dependent on externally defined diets, the result is obsession with food and body image – and excess fat.

In fact, this may be one reason (in addition to processed foods) for the explosion of obesity in the western world. The problem may not be that we all need to go on a diet, but that we are constantly being told that we need to go on a diet, told that we can't trust our own body wisdom.

A POLITICALLY CORRECT PREJUDICE

Not only are we taught to feel guilty about enjoying food, we're taught that how much we weigh is directly related to our value as human beings. This again parallels Victorian attitudes towards sexuality. It promotes the idea that denying one's natural instincts is somehow virtuous. It also creates an intense and culturally sanctioned prejudice against fat people (or even marginally overweight people) that is extremely destructive.

Overweight people are viewed as stupid, lazy, weak-willed, and incompetent. They are discriminated against in the job market and the "love market", and are marginalized, disrespected, insulted, and ignored. This prejudice is so widespread and accepted as reasonable that it appears in earliest childhood. Studies have shown that children as young as 5 years old describe fat children as lazy and stupid, and are less likely to choose them as friends.

Disparaging fat people is the only overt prejudice that is still fully acceptable in polite company. Today, people know that characterizing an entire race or gender as stupid and lazy is ugly and wrong, but (bizarrely) characterizing fat people as stupid and lazy is still perfectly acceptable.

The larger problem is that overweight people internalize these messages, and start to see themselves as disgusting pigs, not worthy of the basic gifts of life. That's why people look at their fat with horror and shame. They're told day in and day out, from earliest childhood, that extra fat is a sign of inadequacy and failure as a human being.

The reason you can't stand the sight of yourself is not because of your fat, per se. It's because of the meaning you give to your fat.

WHAT BEING FAT REALLY MEANS

The solution is to reframe this – stop telling yourself that your fat is shameful and disgusting. It isn't true! Your weight is not a measure of your value as a human being. Character has infinitely more to do with your value as a human being than the shape of your body. The amount of extra fat you carry is vastly overemphasized in this culture, and the meaning the culture gives it is seriously warped.

Carrying extra fat simply means that you have been using food for comfort as well as fuel, because you didn't know how else to deal with the stress and problems in your life. Carrying extra fat is no more shameful than crying. Your fat is like tears; a physical manifestation of distress. If you saw someone crying, you'd view her tears with compassion, not contempt. Your fat is no less a sign of distress, and also deserves to be viewed with compassion rather than contempt.

So when you look in the mirror and see your extra fat, stop your negative self-talk, and instead say to yourself, "This extra fat I'm carrying is not shameful or disgusting, and has no relationship to my value as a human being. It's just a sign that I ate for comfort when I didn't know how to cope with the stress in my life. I'm learning new ways now."

ATTUNED EATING

We are born knowing how to eat normally. An infant knows when she's hungry, and knows when she's had enough. If you try to put food into the mouth of an infant who is no longer hungry, she purses her lips and moves her head from side to side to avoid the spoon.

This body wisdom about what and how much you need to eat is still inside you — you just need to reconnect with it. You don't need a diet to tell you what to eat. Animals in the wild manage to get exactly the nutrition they need. Have you ever seen a fat deer in the woods? We are born with this same body wisdom.

The "Pee" Analogy

The process of feeling hungry, experiencing a body-wisdom-based desire for a certain type of food, eating the food, stopping when satisfied, and then going off to do something else without another thought is "normal eating". This is completely analogous to what occurs when you have to pee. You sense your body's need, you relieve yourself, and then you go back to what you were doing. In both cases, you read a physical signal, meet the physical need, and give it no more thought. That's normal.

Now imagine what a strange world it would be if we were told that peeing had to be done on a schedule. We should pee four times a day, and it should be at four hour intervals, and we should only pee one cup at a time. If we need to pee in between times, we should hold it. If we want to pee more than one cup, we should hold that for the next time. Sound bizarre? That's basically what a diet is. It is just as bizarre to regulate your eating according to arbitrary external rules rather than internal cues.

Eating is a basic bodily function just like elimination. We don't need to be told how to do it.

Control from Within

Eating normally means eating as much as you want whenever you want, but it doesn't mean eating without any limits or control. The difference is that the limits and control come from within. With diets, they come from external rules that are unrelated to hunger, satiation, or how different foods make your body feel.

People with a history of compulsive eating are often so disconnected from their natural internal controls that they don't even know when they're hungry. A primary goal of Normal Eating is to put you back in touch with your own inner wisdom, and show you that you can trust it.

Not the "Eat When Hungry" Diet

Be careful not to turn attuned eating into the "eat when hungry" diet — another set of rules where you white-knuckle your way through cravings, and feel shame and failure if you give in. When you're truly eating normally, you're not fighting with yourself; the craving is gone. Give yourself time. The ability to effortlessly eat only when hungry is where you arrive at the end of the Normal Eating process; it's not where you start.

There are no rules in Normal Eating. There is no failure; there are only learning experiences. Normal Eating is about learning to love yourself, have compassion for your own pain, and practice true self-care so you don't need to self-soothe with food.

Normal Eating Success

When people first find the Normal Eating program, they usually have weight loss as their primary goal. So when they ask whether Normal Eating "works", what they're really asking is whether it will help them lose weight. But weight loss alone does not mean success. If you lose weight by dieting, the obsession just shifts from a desperate desire to lose weight to a desperate fear of regaining it.

Normal Eating success means relief from the mental misery of compulsive urges and self loathing – not constantly worrying about what you should or shouldn't eat, not feeling out of control around food, not obsessing about your weight, not loathing your body, and not putting your life on hold until the day you are finally slim. In fact, you can achieve success in Normal Eating before you ever lose a pound. Once your thinking and behavior change, it can take the body a while to catch up.

You don't have to wait to be slim to experience the joy of Normal Eating success. The feeling of freedom and relief when the obsession lifts is wonderful. What a pleasure it is to just eat normally and stop worrying about it! When you experience this relief, you'll realize that inner freedom is much more important to personal happiness than weight loss per se.

And when you realize this, something ironic happens. As you lose your desperation to lose weight, you become able to honor the needs of your body and eat normally, and your body weight shifts effortlessly towards normal. Normal weight is a side effect of Normal Eating success – an external reflection of inner change. First you think like a thin person, and then, eventually, your body catches up.

The greatest reward of Normal Eating is not the weight loss, though that will happen. It's the peace you gain from resolving core issues and eliminating the obsession with food, eating, and body size.

Recovery is in the Moment

Another common misperception about Normal Eating success is that any episode of emotional eating means failure – that you're either on the beam or off it. But this is not how recovery works. The trigger to eat emotionally is in the moment, overeating is in the moment, and recovery is in the moment.

Each moment that you have an urge to eat for emotional reasons and you resist acting on this urge is a moment of recovery. This pause between urge and action is the very definition of recovery. You have to be able to pause before you can stop! If you experience a craving and pause for 15 minutes before acting on it, you haven't failed. You've experienced 15 minutes of recovery.

Every minute you pause is a victory. In the beginning, your moments of recovery will be spaced out and infrequent. Over time, they will become more and more frequent until moments of recovery outnumber moments of emotional eating. Eventually it will take a major trigger to prompt emotional eating.

You may still occasionally eat for emotional reasons, but don't let that send you into despair. Anybody who has ever used food as an emotional crutch will have a tendency to revert to type when under stress. It doesn't mean you haven't made any progress. With the tools you learn in Normal Eating, you will recognize what's happening, and you'll know how to get back on track quickly.

It helps to stay close to the Normal Eating ideas either by rereading this book or – better yet – joining the Normal Eating Support Group at NormalEating.com. The support group provides a place to share struggles and success, and stay immersed in the Normal Eating ideas. Otherwise the general cultural pressure can lead you back to dieting and weight obsession.

Some Comparisons

There are other attuned eating programs, but Normal Eating is different in some important ways. Here's how Normal Eating compares to three other popular approaches:

- Geneen Roth's Why Weight
- Overcoming Overeating
- Overeater's Anonymous

GENEEN ROTH'S WHY WEIGHT?

Why Weight? A Guide to Ending Compulsive Eating is a book by Geneen Roth. Both the Why Weight and Normal Eating methods are meant to help people overcome compulsive eating, stop dieting, and eat normally, so of course there are some similarities. But there are also some significant differences.

A Focus on Weight Loss

The most important difference is that Why Weight focuses on weight loss as a goal. In fact, this is the biggest difference between Normal Eating and all other non-diet approaches.

Focus on weight loss as the goal is the single biggest reason that the non-diet approach doesn't work for many people. You can't listen to your body and trust what it's telling you if your mind is constantly trying to second guess it.

Lack of Effective Tools

Geneen Roth went through a process of recovery with a therapist and can accurately describe the emotional issues that drive compulsive eating. But she's not a therapist herself, as she's the first to admit. Her expertise is not in helping people to apply this knowledge; she only can describe it. Her descriptions are movingly eloquent – she's a great writer – but a general awareness that you eat, for example, when you're angry does not help you to not eat when you're angry.

The Why Weight suggestion to write essays about each generic trigger (for example, anger) is not an effective tool for recovery. Deep insight about triggers doesn't happen in after-the-fact reflection; it happens in the moment you're experiencing the trigger.

The moment of craving is when you have an opportunity for insight that is actionable. That's why Normal Eating so strongly emphasizes the importance of pausing before acting on an urge to eat. Sitting with the discomfort of the compulsion for long enough to realize what's triggering it is how you get well.

A DESCRIPTION, NOT A MAP

Why Weight and Normal Eating both have four stages, but the only similarity between them is the count. The Why Weight stages simply describe the recovery process – for example, you'll be able to eat when hungry before you can stop when full, and the whole process will take 1-2 years. All true, but that doesn't explain how to get there.

The Normal Eating stages, in contrast, provide tools to move you through the process. They are not just a description of recovery, they are a roadmap for getting there.

These are the Why Weight stages:

1. Acknowledgement there's a problem.

2. Reaction against deprivation.

3. Identifying and solving the problems that cause you to eat compulsively.

4. Joy in recovery.

Stage 3 – identifying and solving the problems that cause you to eat compulsively – is the part that people have trouble with, and the focus of the Normal Eating stages.

It's easy to say "Just eat when you're hungry", but it's very hard to do if you're an emotional eater. An emotional eater has to do a lot of internal work to be able to "just eat when hungry". Most people find it difficult or impossible to do that level of internal work without guidance. This is what Normal Eating provides.

Normal Eating breaks the process into stages, with each stage building on the previous stage. That lets you focus on one thing at a time, which is much more manageable. The exercises at each stage greatly improve your odds of success, as well.

Many people who loved Geneen Roth's books but still couldn't stop eating compulsively find success with Normal Eating.

Overcoming Overeating

The book *Overcoming Overeating: How to Break the Diet / Binge Cycle and Live a Healthier More Satisfying Life* was written by Jane Hirschmann and Carol Munter. It offers some useful insights, but can be enabling and destructive. It overemphasizes "legalizing" formerly forbidden foods, and underemphasizes the development of internal controls that naturally limit what we eat. The result is that people often gain weight without end.

Telling a compulsive eater that she can stop food cravings by unlimited compulsive eating makes about as much sense as telling an alcoholic that he can overcome his craving for alcohol by unlimited drinking!

Deprivation: Just One Piece

Normal Eating used to use the term "Legalizing" to describe Stage 1. This led to widespread misunderstanding because Overcoming Overeating uses the same term very differently. Stage 1 is now called "Reframing" rather than "Legalizing".

In Overcoming Overeating, "legalizing" means eating lots of formerly forbidden foods on the theory that this will remove compulsive urges for these foods. But eating lots of something only removes feelings of deprivation, and deprivation is generally a small piece of why someone eats compulsively.

For most people, the issues that fuel compulsive eating run much deeper. If you eat a lot of a particular food you may tire of it. But if you haven't dealt with the underlying emotional issues, you'll just eat some other food compulsively.

The advice to eat lots of formerly forbidden foods without any attempt at mindfulness or self-control leads to significant weight gain that is never lost.

REFRAMING VS. LEGALIZING

Normal Eating's Stage 1, called "Reframing", is not meant to remove feelings of compulsion. It's the emotional work in Stages 2 and 3 that removes the compulsion.

Reframing is about changing how you think about food – learning that you have the right to eat whatever you want, and becoming able to do this without guilt. You'll probably still be overeating at this stage, but you will stop beating yourself up for it. This prepares you for the work in Stages 2 and 3.

Changing how you think does not require eating foods that you previous avoided. You can know you're free to eat potato chips without actually eating them. Conversely, you can eat potato chips every day, and if you feel guilty every time you do it, you've accomplished nothing.

In Normal Eating, Stage 1 is not something you eat your way through; it's something you think your way through.

OVEREATERS ANONYMOUS

Overeaters Anonymous (OA) is a 12-step program for people who suffer from compulsive overeating. Although most people in OA rely on a rigid food plan, this is not mandated by OA World Services. Theoretically, each person can choose his or her own food plan, and this plan could be Normal Eating.

Normal Eating is very compatible with the OA philosophy. Both focus on curing compulsive eating versus weight loss per se. OA looks to a higher power for help, and Normal Eating looks to body wisdom, which is easily conceived as the voice of a higher power.

In OA terms, Normal Eating could be described this way. Our bodies were created by a higher power – something greater than ourselves. Our bodies have within them knowledge and wisdom that our puny brains can't begin to grasp. Our bodies maintain themselves without any conscious effort or control. Our bodies also know exactly what they need for fuel to survive. They are perfectly tuned detectors.

But body wisdom speaks in a whisper. If we have a lot of noise in our heads from emotional cravings, it can be hard to hear what our bodies are saying. Learning to tune into body wisdom – the voice of our higher power – is a primary goal of Normal Eating. It is also a primary goal of OA.

According to this view, the third step – letting go of our will, and turning it over to a higher power – means listening to our bodies, not our minds. When we ignore our bodies' signals and eat despite pain or discomfort, it's "self-will run amok". People in OA are told to pray for willingness. Applied to Normal Eating, this means praying for the willingness to act in accordance with body wisdom, for the strength and courage to sit with whatever is bothering us, and for the compassion and self-love to live with our choices if we are unable to do it.

GAP IN THEORY VERSUS PRACTICE

Unfortunately, while these ideas are compatible with OA World Services principles, they aren't supported by most OA meetings. OA, as it exists in the real world, says that our higher power is not inside us, and we must look outside of ourselves for guidance and instruction on food choices – that we are fundamentally incapable of making good choices on our own. This attitude, which is antithetical to the principles of Normal Eating, is very much part of the OA culture, if not its doctrine, and makes it hard for people in OA to use Normal Eating as their food plan. Normal Eating is about regaining trust in ourselves, while traditional OA says we cannot trust ourselves at all.

Most people in OA define abstinence as following a rigid food plan where what to eat for the day or week is decided in advance. Ideally this plan gets prior approval from another person (their sponsor). They must ignore all body signals since these are deemed unreliable. They are supposed to call their sponsors for permission to vary even slightly from their food plan. To eat an unplanned and unapproved pickle is considered a "slip".

I think this is a humiliating way to live, completely invalidating. Also, the common OA practice of weighing and measuring each bite of food promotes obsession with food and eating.

DANGERS OF THE DISEASE MODEL

Another problem is the OA disease model. When OA says that compulsive overeaters have "the disease" of compulsive overeating, it's saying compulsive overeaters are essentially flawed and can't trust themselves. I think this view is destructive. Body wisdom (the voice of a higher power) exists in people who eat compulsively as strongly and surely as it exists in everyone else. Anyone can learn to hear the whisper of body wisdom – the voice of our higher power – and act in accordance with it. We can trust ourselves. We are not flawed.

It's very different to say our *actions* are unhealthy versus *we* are unhealthy. If we're just doing something unhealthy, we can stop. But if *we* are unhealthy, we're doomed.

AA adopted the disease model to take the moral judgment out of alcoholism. It was more helpful for alcoholics to see themselves as suffering from a disease than to be branded as morally inferior. But it's possible to go a step further.

People with addictive personalities tend to cope with stress and pain through compulsive or addictive behavior. But that's just a personality style; it's not a disease. There's even an upside to this personality characteristic. People with addictive personalities can be extremely high achieving because of their intense focus when something captures their interest. The flip side of addictive energy is passion.

People with a history of alcohol or drug abuse should abstain entirely from self-prescribed mood- or mind-altering substances. But compulsive eaters can't abstain entirely from eating. When it comes to eating, people must learn to be healthy, and I think they can.

PART 2
COMPULSIVE EATING & SELF-LOVE

THE NATURE OF ADDICTION

Lack of choice – that feeling of being compelled to do what our minds do not choose – is the essence of addiction. Compulsive eating is an addictive behavior, so recovery means being able to choose. The final stage in Normal Eating is Choosing.

The first-ever consistently successful treatment for addiction was Alcoholics Anonymous. AA's great insight was that addiction is not a moral failure. Alcoholics are not morally deficient – able to stop drinking but choosing not to. They have lost the capacity to choose. Willpower gets you nowhere with addiction.

The same is true for compulsive eating. Society says compulsive eaters could stop if they wanted to, that over-eating is a moral failure – gluttony, lack of self-control. But compulsive eating is no more a choice than alcoholism. The way out of compulsive eating is not greater willpower. Plus the shame people feel at being unable to stop just makes the problem worse.

Alcoholics Anonymous described addiction as a "disease" rather than a moral failing, and this view pervades all 12-step programs. As I said in the section on "Overeaters Anonymous", I'm not a fan of the disease model. I don't see addiction as a moral failure, but neither do I see it as a disease.

THE ADDICTIVE PERSONALITY

A tendency towards addictive behavior is a personality style. People with addictive personalities tend to be perfectionist, obsessive, black-and-white thinkers who approach life in an all-or-nothing manner. Moderation does not come naturally – if a little is good, more must be better. People with addictive personalities also tend to be escapist, fleeing from discomfort through obsessive distraction or self-medication.

An addictive personality predisposes you to addiction, but it isn't all bad. Some aspects are quite positive. Think of all the interesting and talented people in public life who had to deal with alcohol or drug problems at some point. The same single-minded focus that made them vulnerable to addiction contributed to their brilliance and success. Both are manifestations of the addictive personality style – in one case it works for them, in another against them.

Addictive patterns similar to the diet-binge cycle can appear in many areas of life. For example, you might alternate between work-a-holism and procrastination. Essentially this is going on a "time diet" where you do nothing but work, followed by a "time binge" where you do no work at all. And then, when the work piles up, you go on another "time diet".

Spending patterns also can mirror the diet-binge cycle. An overly tight budget (a "money diet"), provokes an irresistible urge to spend (a "money binge"), followed by another over-tightening of the budget.

People with addictive personalities can approach anything addictively, and often do. Even reading novels and surfing the internet can become addictive – obsessive distractions from the discomfort of everyday life.

SWITCHING ADDICTIONS

The original AA literature talked about an "allergy" to alcohol. But addiction is not about the substance – food, alcohol, or whatever. An alcoholic isn't only vulnerable to alcohol.

Newly sober alcoholics frequently substitute a new compulsion – eating, romantic obsession, or other drugs. In the early days of AA, so many alcoholics tried to quit drinking by switching to marijuana that they coined a sarcastic term for it: "The Marijuana Maintenance Program". People addicted to drugs like heroin or cocaine frequently quit by switching to alcohol, with the idea that this is safe because they're not alcoholics. But of course they immediately begin drinking alcoholically.

Today, to be considered clean and sober in a 12-step program for drugs or alcohol, you must give up all mood- and mind-altering substances, not just your drug of choice. Even then, an addict remains vulnerable to process addictions like food, sex, and romantic obsession. It's for this reason that newly sober members of AA are advised not to start a new relationship for at least a year. This gives the person time to deal with the core issue of an addictive personality: a resistance to living life on life's terms.

The crucial lesson that a person recovering from addiction must learn is this: *Sometimes in life, you just have to feel bad.* This is crucially important, so I'll say it again: Sometimes in life, you just have to feel bad. The solution to emotional eating isn't to find some other way to never feel bad — some other way to soothe away all discomfort. It's occasionally helpful to take a warm bath or do something else comforting when you feel like eating, but it's not the long-term solution.

The solution to emotional eating is to learn to sit with your feelings. To fix the problems in your life, you must be able to face them and look at them. Sitting with discomfort and feeling your feelings is very hard for someone with an addictive personality, but you *can* learn to do it. If you don't, you'll continue to act on your natural impulse to escape through a binge, a drink, an online game, or whatever else is handy.

You may be able to stop addictive behavior for a while by willpower alone, but it's not pleasant. The cravings remain, and the inability to deal with life on life's terms remains. AA calls this a "dry drunk". The equivalent for compulsive eaters is a restrictive diet or Overeaters Anonymous food plan. In fact, there's a book by Becky Lu Jackson called *Dieting: A Dry Drunk*.

True recovery from compulsive eating does not involve a lifetime of weighing and measuring every bite you eat. True recovery from compulsive eating requires getting to the bottom of what's triggering you and dealing with it. That's what releases you from the compulsion.

NORMAL DRINKING?

Compulsive eaters have a higher-than-average tendency to abuse alcohol. The reason is simple: compulsive eaters have addictive personalities, and thus easily switch from one compulsion to another (see the chapter on "The Nature of Addiction"). Some years ago, someone posted a question in the Normal Eating Support Group that sent a jolt through me:

> I've been experimenting with different types of wines, imported beers, etc., and making it part of the Reframing process. I usually have at least three glasses of wine or beer. Though I can stop on the fourth glass, I've been feeling like drinking every day. Has anybody else been through this? Is there any way to apply the

> Normal Eating tools to achieve "normal drinking" or can only AA help me?

Someone else responded with this:

> I am also a social drinker, but since beginning Reframing I have started to gradually up my intake and allow myself 2-3 glasses of wine every night.

Until I read these posts, it never dawned on me that people might try to apply Normal Eating ideas to alcohol. I'm grateful it came up because it's an extremely dangerous idea, and I wouldn't have thought to address it otherwise.

To be clear: *Alcohol is a drug. It is not a food. Normal Eating principles are not applicable to drug use.*

Even people who don't have a problem with alcohol should use it minimally when working on Normal Eating. Alcohol lowers inhibitions and impairs judgment, making it more likely you'll overeat. Alcohol also blurs full conscious awareness of your experience, and mindfulness is an important element of the Normal Eating recovery process. You will make faster progress if your drinking is minimal.

Plus alcohol is a poison that has to be detoxified by the liver and offers no nutrition whatsoever. It depletes you rather than feeds you. It's worse than just empty calories. Many people don't drink at all because it seems like a silly thing to do – Donald Trump has never had a drink in his life.

Note: If cutting down on how much you drink or temporarily stopping feels like a big hardship and out of the question, it's a strong indication that you have a problem with alcohol and should stop drinking completely.

If you have any question in your mind whether alcohol may be a problem for you, I strongly urge you to try an AA meeting and see how it feels. To find a meeting near you, look up the number for Alcoholics Anonymous in your local phone book, or get a meeting list for your town on the internet.

You don't have to commit to anything to go to an AA meeting, and if it's right for you, you'll love it. You'll feel like you're home at last. AA is a wonderful fellowship filled with warm, honest people who understand you, support you, and don't judge you.

Compulsive Eating

Society characterizes overeating as "self-indulgence" – giving yourself more pleasure than you have a right to. This is an element of the stigma against fat people. But how much fun is it, really, to eat to the point of discomfort? What is self-indulgent about inflicting pain upon yourself?

Being overfull is uncomfortable. Your distended stomach presses against your internal organs and makes it hard to breathe. Loosening your waistband doesn't help because the pressure is on the inside. You feel sluggish, your stomach hurts. Plus excess food is ultimately stored as excess fat, making you unhappy on a whole other level.

Normal eaters are the true "self-indulgers" because they eat in a way that maximizes their pleasure – both in the moment, and in the long-term.

When you eat past full, there's a part of you that keeps saying, "I'm really full, I want to stop eating so I won't be uncomfortable, but I can't!" Eating past full isn't a deliberate act of self-indulgence. It's a compulsive behavior that you don't feel you have the ability to stop, even though you want to.

Eating compulsively feels insane. You're doing something that you don't want to do. So why are you doing it?

WHY PEOPLE EAT COMPULSIVELY

People eat compulsively because it fills important needs that they don't know how else to fill. Diets don't work because they ask you to give up food as a crutch without providing anything in its place. You can't just decide to live without having your needs met. The pressure from internal distress eventually pushes you to seek relief in the only way you know how: eating.

Compulsive eating meets emotional needs in two primary ways:

- As a distraction from what's really bothering you – a way to flee conscious awareness of life problems that you fear will overwhelm you, push you beyond your ability to cope.

- As a way to comfort yourself (and rebel!) when you feel trapped in a bad situation with no power to change it – a way to cope with feeling victimized.

When you can surface what's really bothering you in the moment – not in a general way, but specifically – the urge to eat goes away because you no longer need the functions it serves. Your need for a distraction evaporates once the problem enters conscious awareness. And once you have conscious awareness of the true problem, you can explore your options so you no longer feel trapped and powerless.

People often don't see their options, but no matter how difficult a situation is, there are always options. The prerequisite for finding them is allowing the problem into conscious awareness. You can't find solutions to problems that you won't allow yourself to think about! Let it in. Our fear of something is always worse than the reality of it.

Normal Eating works because it doesn't ask you to live with unmet needs. Instead it helps you to discover what needs you're filling with food, and guides you to find other, more authentic ways to meet those needs. If you're using food to cope with a non-hunger problem, there is always something else you can do that will work better than eating. The only problem for which food is the best solution is physical hunger.

THE BIG EMPTY

Addiction is sometimes called the "disease of more". An addicted person always wants more of whatever they're addicted to. No amount of food is enough for a compulsive eater, just as no amount of alcohol is enough for an alcoholic.

The problem – the root cause of this insatiability – is trying to fill a need with something that can't satisfy the need. So no matter how much you have it's not enough; the need remains. If your foot itches and you scratch your nose, it will never satisfy.

Sometimes the need can feel very amorphous – just a vague sense of emptiness inside, that something is lacking or missing. You hear this described by virtually every person in recovery for addiction. I call it the "Big Empty". It's this hole inside – the Big Empty – that that addicts try to fill with "more".

So what does satisfy? What can fill the hole? The answer – an insight from the 12-step world – is a sense of spiritual connection. This doesn't have to mean religious faith or even a belief in God. In the most generic terms, a spiritual connection means a sense that you have a place in the world, that you are an integral part of all that is.

A sense of spiritual connection removes the feeling every addict has of being different from everyone else, separate and apart (or as AA puts it, "terminally unique"). This feeling of separateness and alienation is what causes the Big Empty. A sense of spiritual connection, however you conceive it, fills this hole and allows you put down your "drug of choice" (food, alcohol, or whatever).

In the *I Ching,* an ancient Chinese book of wisdom, there's a passage in the hexagram "Corners of the Mouth (Providing Nourishment)" that I've always liked. From the Wilhelm/Baynes translation: "He who seeks nourishment that does not nourish reels from desire to gratification, and in gratification craves desire." That's a great description of what happens with addiction. In addiction, you look to solve a problem with a substance or behavior that doesn't have the power to solve the problem. So no matter how much of it you have or do, it's never enough.

IT'S NEVER ABOUT THE FOOD

In case you're still thinking that compulsive eating has something to do with enjoying food too much, I'll end this chapter with a story posted in the Normal Eating Support Group. It is unedited:

> My sister has lost 88 lbs since October. Her secret? She quit dieting. She also found what works - happiness!
>
> Okay, a bit of background. My sister is mentally handicapped and was married to a mentally handicapped man for three years. She gained 150 lbs in that time. Part of it was from having unlimited access to food for the first time in her life. Her husband would bring home a 15 piece bucket of fried chicken for dinner and the two of them would eat the whole thing. She would bake a cake for dessert and they would eat it all in one day. Like kids turned loose in a candy store.
>
> But part of the problem was that everyone was trying to "help" her lose weight. She weighed close to 350 lbs,

doctors put her on special diets and diet pills, social workers sent nutritionists to work with her, my mom and I paid for her to do Weight Watchers, friends and family emailed her low-calorie recipes, people stocked her cabinets with diet foods - a classic case of leading a horse to water but not being able to make them drink! She gained 40 lbs while following everyone's diet advice.

However the real problem wasn't what she was eating, but what was eating her. She was very unhappy. Her husband was cruel - called her a big fat pig all day (while he was bringing her donuts and fried chicken), she was very isolated from others, very lonely and bored out of her skull. Because of her weight she also was pretty immobile; she couldn't get up into the public buses to go anywhere and had no other means of transportation. She could barely walk to the mailbox and back. I am certain everyone's constant attention to her weight and attempts to help control her eating just added to the problem.

But in October, she got divorced from her very unhappy marriage, she moved back to a group home where she had friends, activities, and a fulfilling job. The weight has fallen off since - with no outside help and no effort on her own part. She was just finally happy again for the first time in years! She no longer is looking to food to fill the gaps in her life - she has filled those with "living". Last month she walked a mile for Race for the Cure, and this month she participated in Special Olympics and ran the 100 meter dash.

Anyway - this just underscored for me again that weight problems really aren't about food. In most cases they are about being unhappy in some way. And the cure isn't dieting - it is fixing whatever is making us so unhappy!

Fat Can Serve a Function

I've talked about how eating compulsively can serve a need. It may surprise you to learn that being fat also can serve a need – especially for women. Have you ever wondered why seeing a lower number on the scale triggers you to overeat? It's because of ambivalence about being slim. Resistance to losing weight is ironic after wanting it so badly for so long, but it's very common.

Most women, when asked if they want to be fat, will quickly say no. But it makes life easier in some ways. Being fat:

- Reduces unwanted sexual attention and advances.

71

- Focuses workplace attention away from a woman's appearance and onto her performance.

- Makes friendships with other women easier because a fat woman is not a threat.

- Allows women to bond with their mothers and other women over a shared problem.

- Allows women to test a man's affections and make sure they are based on substance.

- Is a way to rebel against and reject women's role in society.

- Makes women feel less vulnerable and "easy to push around".

- Reduces discomfort with intimacy by making it less likely to happen.

- Is a way to express anger and resentment towards a partner.

- Reduces anxiety in women who fear their own tendency toward promiscuity by reducing opportunity.

- Provides a symbolic "thick skin" so women feel less exposed.

- Reduces pressure to perform by lowering other's expectations (playing on fat prejudice).

- Provides an excuse to put off actions that are challenging or scary.

- Can convey low self-esteem, telling ourselves and the world we are no good.

RELATIONSHIPS AND SEXUALITY

Body size and sexuality are highly interrelated because, well, we have sex with our bodies! Fear of sexual and emotional intimacy – whatever the cause – can trigger overwhelming anxiety. Weight gain is an effective way to quell this anxiety because it reduces the chance that the intimacy we fear will occur.

Fat also puts a physical barrier around us that can give a feeling a safety. A high percentage of people who were sexually abused as children are significantly overweight as adults. For a vulnerable child who can't say no, what better way to keep people away? That feeling of being helpless to say no often continues into adulthood, though as adults we do have the power to say no.

Fat can serve as symbolic protection against other types of invasion, as well. People who are overweight frequently have difficulty saying no in general, and setting boundaries. It's harder to "push someone around" when she weighs 200 pounds. Many formerly overweight women feel uncomfortably vulnerable when they are smaller.

Then there are the problems that come with being pretty. A pretty woman may wonder whether a man loves her for who she is, or is just enchanted with her appearance. If the man is mainly entranced with her looks, then what will happen when she gets old? What will happen when her skin wrinkles? What if she gains 30 pounds after menopause? What if she gets sick? Is he going to stick by her, or is he going to leave her for someone younger and slimmer? If she gains the 30 pounds now, she doesn't have to wonder. She won't attract men whose main interest is her appearance.

Even walking down the street can be unpleasant for a pretty woman. Comments, catcalls, and pickup attempts may be flattering to some, but others find it invasive and disrespectful. It's presumptuous and demeaning for a man to walk up to a woman on the street who he doesn't know and say "Give me a smile, honey", as though she's a child who exists only for his entertainment. This problem is easily eliminated by gaining weight. Then a woman can walk down the street unmolested.

PUTTING YOUR LIFE ON HOLD

Another important payoff that fat can provide applies equally to men and women. Fat is a handy excuse for not fully participating in life. People say they'll take a painting class when they're not fat, they'll go back to school when they're not fat, they'll go to the beach when they're not fat, they'll buy new clothes when they're not fat, etc.

Partly this comes from feelings of shame and self-loathing. You deny yourself a full and happy life because you're fat. But often the causation goes the other way. It's not that you're avoiding certain activities because you're fat, but that you're fat as an excuse to avoid certain activities. Also, because of society's prejudice, being fat is a way to lower people's expectations of you, reducing the pressure to perform.

Staying fat can be a way to hide out from life – a way to avoid testing your true capabilities, trying new things, taking risks, and exposing yourself to potential failure. But where there's no risk, there's no reward, either.

TAKING BACK YOUR POWER

It can be hard to uncover the hidden payoffs to being fat. One way is to imagine yourself thin in different situations and see what comes up. Here is a fantasy posted by a woman in the Normal Eating Support Group:

> I walk around proud of myself yet feeling bad because I'm probably making my friends feel self-conscious because they're not as thin as me. I am wearing fitted clothes that show off my thinness. I participate in the activities and laugh and giggle a lot, but in the back of my mind, I feel bad for feeling superior to the other girls who are not as thin as me, and I wish that they wouldn't look at me because I think it's my fault that they're feeling bad about their bodies.

The feelings uncovered in this fantasy highlight a classic female dilemma. Women are taught not to be competitive, not to be powerful, and to take care of everybody else's feelings. They also are taught that they are worthless unless they look a certain way (which includes being thin). But looking that way is such an extreme cultural mandate that achieving it gives a woman power. It makes her a winner in an intensely competitive arena, and generates widespread discomfort and envy in other women. Hmmm... Didn't I just say our culture teaches that women should not be powerful, should not compete, and should not make other people uncomfortable? See the problem?

The crazy culture we live in puts mutually exclusive demands upon women. If we look the way we're supposed to look, we violate a whole bunch of other cultural mandates. Discomfort with personal power and guilt at making others envious are common reasons why many women carry a little extra weight. They're more comfortable sharing the weight problem with their friends than being the target of their envy.

WEIGHT AS SELF-EXPRESSION

One of the reasons for staying fat that I listed at the beginning of this chapter was "low self-esteem". This is because how we look is an integral part of our identity. It's not that how we look affects how we feel about ourselves, it's the reverse. How we look matches our self-assessment. If our deepest private assessment of ourselves is "fat slob", then that is how we will look. You can't think about yourself in that way, and still choose to give yourself the gift of an attractive body.

Weight loss is more than just a transformation of your appearance, it's a transformation of your sense of self. There is nothing you can change about your appearance that's more profoundly transformative than weight loss. If you started off very heavy, people may not even recognize you.

There's a psychological transformation, as well. Some women in the Normal Eating Support Group have talked about feelings of grief as they lose weight, and anxiety about not knowing who they'll be when they're no longer fat. As you lose weight, the old self that you know and are comfortable with is "dying" – thus the grief. And who is the slim "you"? You'll need to find out.

I once had an interesting conversation about this with a woman who'd lost over 100 pounds. She said that her plateaus as she lost weight allowed her to adjust psychologically to each new phase in her appearance. She needed time to grow into becoming a different version of herself.

Once you understand the aspects of being slim that make you uncomfortable, you can take back the power you are giving to your fat. If you're afraid you won't say no to sex, you can learn how to be more assertive. If you're afraid to take risks and try new things, you can learn to feel the fear and do it anyway. If you're afraid of intimacy, you can work to improve your self-esteem (see the chapter on "How to Love Yourself").

Healthy Boundaries

Just by virtue of being a human being, you have certain rights and ownerships that are yours absolutely – things that are in your realm, and over which you have exclusive authority to exercise control. If someone tries to control something that is in your realm, or take something that is yours to give and not theirs to take, that's a *boundary violation*.

When people have trouble setting boundaries – when they let others bully, insult, or take advantage of them – they may create symbolic boundaries around themselves with fat. When you learn to create boundaries through healthy assertiveness, you no longer need fat to protect you.

YOUR RIGHTS

What do you and you alone have rightful authority over?

To begin with, you have absolute right over anything to do with your body. Your body is 100% in your realm; no one but you has any rights pertaining to your body. If someone touches your body without your consent, it's a boundary violation. Obviously rape is a boundary violation, but casual touch can be, too. If someone hugs you when you don't want to be hugged, that is a boundary violation. You have the right to say no to any touch at any time.

When someone tries to control what you eat, it's a boundary violation. How you choose to nourish your body is no one's business but your own. If you want to eat chocolate chip cookies for breakfast, lunch, and dinner, that is your right. That may not be responsible self-care over the long term, but it's your right to do it.

You do not forfeit your rights with self-destructive behavior.

You might ask, "If I'm doing something self-destructive, doesn't someone who loves me have the right to say some-thing?" Yes, they have the right to say something *once*. Saying something once is giving information. But saying something more than once is an attempt to control. They teach this in Al-Anon (a fellowship for people involved with alcoholics). The alcoholic has every right to drink himself to death if that's what he wants to do. It's his body and his life. And anyway, we all know how well nagging works. Did anyone ever get you to stop overeating by nagging you about it?

In addition to having rights over anything related to your body, you have the right to provide what you need for your own happiness, as long as doing so does not impinge on anyone else's rights. This part often confuses people. Where do your rights end and another's begin?

It would take a long time to give a thorough answer to this question, but one thing is for sure: If someone wants something from you, their mere wanting it does *not* give them a right to it. If accommodating someone's request comes at a personal cost to you, you have the right to say no. And if the cost is high enough to harm you, you have the responsibility to say no.

YOUR RESPONSIBILITIES

With rights come responsibilities. It's your responsibility to assert your rights, defend the boundaries of your realm, and not allow invasion. This responsibility is the foundation of self-care, and is neglected at your peril. Nothing feels worse than allowing your boundaries to be violated. It's a major source of unhappiness in life, and a primary reason that people get fat. It is your responsibility as an adult to set clear and firm boundaries with the people in your life.

Some people are incorrigible, but most times they violate our boundaries simply because we let them. We don't defend our rights and ownerships in a firm, clear way. When we fail to set boundaries, people take what's rightly ours – our right to choose, our right to please ourselves, our rights of ownership.

Setting a boundary isn't something you do with great upset and emotion. It's something you do quietly, firmly, clearly, and consistently. If, for example, a family member criticizes you for eating a dessert, you can simply say, "What I eat is my business. Please don't comment on what I eat." Then every time they comment on your eating, set the boundary again. Eventually they will stop.

When you first start setting boundaries after years of allowing people to push you around, make inappropriate comments, and take advantage of you, you will encounter resistance. But this passes. In the end, your relationships will improve, and so will your confidence and self-esteem. Life feels much better when others respect your boundaries.

THE IMPORTANCE OF SELF-CARE

Harshness towards yourself, lack of compassion for your own pain, and unwillingness to act on your own behalf are major reasons why people overeat. If you won't take steps to provide for your own happiness, eating is the only relief you have. To eat normally, you must learn to meet your needs in other areas of life.

Ignoring your own needs is part of a behavior pattern called *codependency*. Though first observed in the cohabitants of chemically dependent people (thus the name), codependency doesn't have anything to do with addicts or addiction. There are many aspects of codependency, but the core problem is lack of self-care. Codependents have weak boundaries, and take care of everybody but themselves.

Compulsive eaters almost always have significant codependency issues. Also, both compulsive eating and codependency are more common in women, perhaps because women are trained from birth to please and take care of others.

YOUR SACRED RIGHT TO HAPPINESS

Emotional eaters may neglect their needs and well-being because they mistakenly think they have no right to time and attention, or that self-care is selfish. Or their self-esteem simply may be so low that they don't think they're worth the bother.

In fact, self-care is not only your right, it's a sacred responsibility. Life is a gift. To not embrace this gift by treasuring your life, protecting your physical and emotional well-being, and enjoying your time on Earth, is to disrespect the gift! You were not put here to suffer. What you want and need are just as important as what other people want and need. You have the right to be happy.

I've mentioned that compulsive eaters tend to be out of touch with their internal cues for hunger and satiation. They also tend to be out of touch with their other feelings and needs. Why be aware of your needs if they aren't going to be met? Better to pretend to yourself and others that you have no needs. If you ignore your feelings and needs for long enough, you become unaware of them.

Normally people know when their needs are unmet or their boundaries are violated by monitoring how they feel. Uncomfortable feelings signal a problem that needs to be addressed. For example, anger is the natural response to a boundary violation. Since codependents and compulsive eaters ignore their own needs, they tend also to ignore the feelings that signal unmet needs. The result? They feel unhappy, but with no idea why.

If you don't know what's bothering you, you can't fix the problem. So how do you feel better? Food is one easy solution. Alcohol is another. In Stage 2 of Normal Eating, you will work on reconnecting with all aspects of your inner self.

MEETING YOUR OWN NEEDS

Airline safety instructions tell parents to put on their own oxygen masks before helping their children put on theirs. There's a reason for this. If the parent passes out or dies, she can't help her child. This principle applies in all areas of life.

It is not selfish to take care of yourself and make sure that your needs are met. In fact, in some ways it's selfish not to. To be the best possible "you" and a giving participant in the world, you must be well and whole. If you're miserable and full of unmet needs, your ability to give is severely hampered.

You have a responsibility to provide for your own self-care and happiness. This is the primary responsibility of every adult. It is no one else's job to monitor your needs and make sure they are met. Nor is it your job to do this for someone else. If you don't take action to meet your own needs, they will go unmet, and your ability to give to others – for example, your children – will be compromised.

If you're a parent, and especially if you're a mother, there's another issue. Mothers need to model good self-care for their children. Boys need to learn through example that women have the right to take care of themselves so they treat their partners respectfully. Girls need to see that women have the right to take care of themselves so they don't sacrifice their lives to someone else's needs.

Part of good self-care is not overburdening yourself with responsibilities that belong to another adult. Giving more than you can "afford" will harm you, and harm your relationship with the person you're trying to help because you'll come to feel resentful. Plus it's not necessary. If you step back and allow space for others to take responsibility, they will. You don't have to do everything yourself.

TAKE AN ACTION

If eating is the most enjoyable part of your day – if it's the only thing you do that is relaxing, enjoyable, and just for you – then you will have a hard time giving up emotional eating. You don't need a perfect life to eat normally, but you do need other sources of pleasure in your life – for example, a hobby.

I'm a big believer in hobbies. I've always had them, and they bring me much joy. Studies have found that people with hobbies are happier than people without hobbies. So what interests you?

HOW TO LOVE
YOURSELF

The pervasive cultural message that fat people are less-than is a poison that gets inside you, and doesn't leave with weight loss. If you don't feel good about yourself when you're fat, you won't feel good about yourself when you're thin, either. In fact, losing weight is almost impossible unless you feel good about yourself to start.

Self-care is a prerequisite for eating normally, but it's hard to take care of yourself when you don't value yourself. Happily, there's a way to break out of this trap. It starts with self-acceptance.

TRUE SELF ACCEPTANCE

People commonly misunderstand "self-acceptance" to mean "no improvements needed". This fundamental error – that you must be perfect and flawless to be acceptable – causes a myriad of problems.

If you only can love yourself if you're flawless, then you become invested in denying your flaws. And if you won't admit your flaws, then you can't change them. Conversely, if you admit your flaws but hate yourself for them, you can't change because you don't like yourself. Change requires self-love because it's such hard work. You won't be willing to put that much effort into improving the life of someone you don't love.

Self-acceptance is not a matter of convincing yourself that you're beautiful and perfect in all respects. True self-acceptance means feeling good about yourself despite your flaws, imperfections, and mistakes. All human beings are flawed, imperfect, and mistake-prone, so it's irrational to require or expect anything else of yourself.

The way to accept your body, even with extra fat, isn't to convince yourself that your fat is good. The way to accept your body is to see what's good about it and what's bad, and be okay with that. If you have a healthy loving relationship with a partner, you don't see him or her as perfect. You know your partner has foibles and imperfections, but that doesn't change your love. Nor (most likely) does your partner have a perfect body, but that's doesn't change your desire. The type of acceptance you feel towards a partner you love is the same type of acceptance you need towards yourself.

For all these reasons, as you might guess, I'm not in favor of "affirmations" that deny obvious reality. In fact, I think they're unhealthy, because your unconscious knows the truth and knows you're rejecting yourself. Still, it does matter what you say when you talk to yourself.

Monitor Your Self-Talk

There is a constant stream of silent talk in your head, and chances are that a lot of what you say to yourself isn't very nice. Negative self-talk keeps you stuck. Stop yelling at yourself, stop saying mean things to yourself, stop calling yourself names, stop telling yourself you're useless or stupid or incompetent or whatever it is that you say to yourself. This is self-abuse, and reinforces low self-esteem.

The moment you notice negative self-talk, stop it and correct it. If you catch your reflection in a store window and spontaneously insult yourself, stop yourself mid-thought and tell yourself something different. For example: "The amount of fat on my body does not define my value as a human being." or "The extra fat on my body just means that I sometimes eat to self-soothe – a visual manifestation of internal pain."

It's extremely important that you do this, and do it consistently. Don't ever allow yourself to engage in negative self-talk. Don't go down that road. If you can't think of anything positive to say instead, just say to yourself, "Stop" and shift your attention elsewhere.

You can change how you feel by changing how you think, and it starts with self-talk.

SMALL ACTS OF SELF-CARE

Of all the things you can do to improve self-esteem, the most powerful is to take self-loving actions, no matter how small. What you say to yourself has an effect, but actions speak even louder than words.

When you treat yourself in ways that imply you matter and have value, your unconscious observes it and your feelings about yourself spontaneously improve. You just feel better. You can't talk yourself into loving yourself. But if you act like you love yourself (even if you don't), then your feelings change to match your actions.

When you're feeling low, an act of self-care can feel virtually impossible, but you can start small. Pick something you can do in less than 15 minutes that improves your life in some small way. Put clean sheets on your bed, or take a walk. Each time you take a self-loving action, your unconscious notices and says, "Hmm... I'm treating myself like I have some value. I must have some value."

The more you do it, the better you'll feel about yourself, and the easier it will be to take more self-loving actions. Eventually, self-respect and self-care will become part of who you are and how you live your life.

PART 3
THE NORMAL EATING METHOD

Getting Started

When an emotional eater stops dieting and starts eating according to body wisdom, she goes through a process. This large shift in thoughts, feelings, and actions requires new skills and learning in many areas. That's why so many people who have read other books on attuned eating are unable to implement the ideas.

Normal Eating brings the goal within reach by breaking the process into manageable stages. Each stage has learning objectives that build upon the previous stage. What you learn in Stage 1 prepares you for Stage 2, what you learn in Stage 2 prepares you for Stage 3, and what you learn in

Stage 3 prepares you for Stage 4. Learning one new set of skills at a time greatly improves your odds of success.

BE PATIENT WITH YOURSELF

Don't try to rush the process. That's everybody's impulse in the beginning, but it will not get you where you want to go. If you try to move ahead to a stage you're not yet ready for, you'll just discourage yourself and set yourself back. Work on each stage in order and don't try to jump ahead.

Normal Eating is not a quick fix program. The emotional work required for long-lasting change is deep and intense, and cannot be rushed. On average it takes people one to two years to work through the stages, with Stage 3 being the most difficult.

If compulsive overeating were easy to fix, no one would have the problem! So go slow, take baby steps, and give yourself time to do the hard work.

GET SUPPORT

Learning to eat normally is difficult, all the more so because listening to your body is not the culturally approved way to deal with weight problems. So make sure you have support as you work through the stages. This can be an understanding therapist, a friend moving through the stages with you, or the Normal Eating Support Group (online at NormalEating.com). The online support group can be very helpful. Here are quotes from three members:

There is so much wisdom here. I have found it so helpful to read through the forum - it's incredible that almost every feeling and every struggle I've had has been discussed somewhere on the board. In addition to reading valuable strategies to help you work through the stages, there is honesty, joy, pain, all the feelings that we try to articulate.

I noticed this morning as I was browsing, lurking among several of the threads and posts that having each other's feedback helps us not feel guilty for what we are doing. So many of us have common thoughts and issues. The whole camaraderie opens up the door of self acceptance. Having this forum allows us to be set free from isolation and self loathing. We are given a chance to compare and recognize that it isn't just ME that feels this way or has this vague confusion.

I really don't know what I'd do without this board. I realised recently that I no longer compulsively search the net for the ANSWER to my eating disorder. I just come here and read and write and get the reminders I need to keep me heading towards FREEDOM.

IT'S PROGRESS, NOT PERFECTION

It's natural to zigzag a bit as you move through the stages – two steps forward, one step back. Each stage has a key learning on which the next stage builds, but you don't have to do a stage perfectly in order to move on. You learn a few skills at a time so you are not overwhelmed, but you may occasionally need to shift your focus back to previously learned skills.

Finally, please remember that eating mainly in response to hunger is where you arrive at the *end* of this process; it's not where you start in Stage 1. If you could eat only when hungry just by deciding to, then you wouldn't need the Normal Eating program!

Your Weight
History

As soon as you can find a quiet hour, you should write your weight history – really a weight and eating history, but I call it a weight history for short. Writing your weight history in the Normal Eating style can give surprising insights into your eating triggers.

The basic idea is to think back on your life, starting at the time when your weight first became an issue. List the times when you gained or lost 10 or more pounds, and what was happening in your life at the time. If there were periods when your eating wasn't normal but your weight was stable

– for example, if you were purging – then include that in the history as well.

Your weight history can give important insights into your main triggers for emotional eating. You might find, for example, that you gain weight when you feel trapped and victimized, and lose weight when you feel competent and effective. Or you may gain weight when you feel unloved, and lose weight when you feel loved. Or both.

But don't try to figure this out while you're writing the history!

The tricky part in writing a weight history is getting around the brain's relentless urge to interpret before having all the facts. People tend to have preconceived ideas about their eating, such as "I gain weight when I'm unhappy". These preconceptions can prevent you from seeing deeper motivations or learning anything new.

WRITE TWO PARALLEL HISTORIES

There are two common errors people make when writing their weight histories. The first is to focus exclusively on their eating and write little or nothing about what else was happening in their lives. The second is trying to figure out the reasons for their eating while they are still writing. Neither approach will yield new insights.

What works best is to write two parallel histories – your eating and your life – in summary form rather than a long narrative, and without interpreting as you write unless it's something you were aware of at the time. For example, if you started purging after a boyfriend made a comment about your body, that's important to mention since it was in your head at the time. But leave out any after-the-fact interpretations.

Use this general format to create the summary. Put the year, your age, and your weight as a section header, and then write what was happening with your eating and – totally separate – what was happening in your life. Don't try to connect the two:

Year:_____ age:_____ weight:_____

- What your eating was like (normal, bingeing, purging, dieting, obsessive weighing, etc.).

- The major events in your life at the time, apart from eating and weight, and how they made you feel. Don't leave out how they made you feel because your feelings are what drive emotional eating.

Be brief! For each time period, write just a sentence or two about your eating and weight, and another sentence or two about the major events in your life at the time. If you write too much, the patterns will be obscured under detail.

Take time to think back and remember, and only write down the major events. Note that what makes an event "major" is how strongly it affected your feelings about yourself or your life. Something that sounds small, like losing a friendship, can be a major event.

Any time your weight went up or down more than 10 pounds, or you started or stopped purging, or your degree of weight obsession changed, create a new entry with year, age, and weight. You can group together years when your eating and weight were stable.

If weight became an issue for you in adolescence, start there. If you were fat as a child, then you need to start earlier. Whenever you start, go year by year from there to the present, remembering your life.

If you're middle-aged, you may have to refer to résumés or other records to recall what you were doing at different ages. Once you remember what you were doing – the job, the school, the child – you'll remember your frame of mind, and (inevitably) what you weighed. Most people who have eating and weight issues can remember what they weighed at any given time if they think about it long enough to remember what they were doing.

It takes some time to do a thorough weight history, but it's time well spent. The insights you gain can provide important clues when you're trying to figure out what's bothering you in real time.

INTERPRETATION

After you've finished writing the history – and only after – go back and reread it for patterns. You may think you won't learn anything new, but you will. You'll see connections between life events and emotional eating that you didn't notice before, and you'll start to recognize themes.

It can be useful to make a table or graph of your weight year by year, with a brief note next to each year about what was happening. This can make the patterns really jump out at you. But it's not necessary to do this – you'll see patterns just from reading it over.

I learned from my own weight history that being in a bad situation per se didn't trigger emotional eating. I was sometimes in terrible situations and yet ate normally. What triggered emotional eating was feeling trapped in a bad situation. If I felt I had options, my weight was stable. But if I felt trapped, I used food to rebel and comfort myself. I later discovered that I wasn't the only one triggered by feeling trapped in a bad situation. This is the single most common reason for emotional eating.

In the early days of the Normal Eating Support Group, I posted feedback for people on their weight histories. Eventually there were just too many people to keep doing this. But if you look in the forum archives, you'll see examples of weight histories and how to interpret them.

Many support group members still post their weight histories to get feedback from their peers. You may feel you want to do this, but write your weight history first for yourself, without the idea that you will post it. If you're thinking that others will read it, you may censor yourself and remove important details. Decide after you finish whether you're comfortable posting it and getting feedback.

If you do post your weight history, don't forget to mention how tall you are. A given weight could be heavy or light, depending on your height.

STAGE 1: REFRAMING

People who are overweight can feel they have no right to eat at all, let alone eat so-called "fattening foods". Chronic dieting also can make certain foods feel taboo and off-limits. Both engender feelings of deprivation that can trigger reactive eating.

And then there is the real deprivation of poverty. A woman in the Normal Eating Support Group posted at length about her experiences growing up without enough food to eat. Today she has plenty, but the feelings of deprivation remain and affect her eating.

Feelings of deprivation create noise in your head that drown out the whisper of body wisdom. So in Stage 1 of

Normal Eating, you eliminate feelings of deprivation by **reframing your thinking** about food. To the extent that deprivation has been driving your eating, reframing will reduce compulsion. But for most people, the causes of emotional eating are much more complex, so don't expect all compulsive eating to stop in Stage 1.

The goal in Stage 1 is limited: to understand that all foods are available to you. You have the right to eat whatever you want, and there is no reason for guilt or shame.

Think about what it means to feel guilty. You feel guilty when you've done something morally wrong – something you don't have the right to do. But you have the right to make whatever eating choices you want. You even have the right to make unhealthy choices if you want. Eating is an issue of self-care, not moral correctness.

EATING AND SLEEPING

An analogy can make this easier to see. Your body needs sleep as well as nutrition. Do you feel wracked with guilt and shame if you stay up all night? You may feel annoyed with yourself when you're tired the next day, but you don't feel guilt and shame. You know that it's your right to stay up all night if you choose, even if it's not the best choice for your health.

It's the same with eating. You have the right to eat whatever you want, whenever you want, and however much you want. You are responsible for your own self-care, but your right to choose what you eat is absolute. There's nothing to feel guilty about.

If, at a given moment, you decide that the comfort you'll get from eating is more important to you than the stomachache afterwards or any other consequence, then you have the right to do it. But you also must take responsibility for what you've freely chosen. If you choose to eat because you're depressed, then don't go the self-recrimination route afterwards. You decided to do it, you did it, and that's that.

It's very important to know on a deep level that what you eat is entirely your choice. In dieting and rebellion eating, you not only deny your right to make your own food choices, but also your responsibility for your food choices. You can't choose to nourish your body responsibly (the goal in Stage 4) until you know on a deep level that what you eat is entirely your choice, for better or for worse.

DON'T SNEAK FOOD

Don't sneak food, and don't avoid eating in front of other people. Hiding your eating, or eating on the sly while driving or standing, are acts of guilt and shame. Sit down at the table to eat; eat in public. You have the right to eat whatever you want, no matter what your weight. It is your body. If anyone tries to criticize you, set a boundary. What you eat is your choice and your business (see the chapter on "Healthy Boundaries" for more).

EAT MINDFULLY

Pay attention to what you're eating. Don't eat in front of the television or while reading so you're hardly aware of your eating experience. When you eat, focus on the experience of eating. Eat whatever you want, but do it slowly, deliberately, and consciously. Stay present. Look at each bite before it enters your mouth; smell it. Be aware of how the food feels and tastes in your mouth. Also notice how your body feels. Be aware of all your body sensations while you eat. Really focus on it – even close your eyes if this helps.

In Stage 2 you will explore your eating experience in more specific ways, but for right now, just practice mindfulness. Do you like what you're eating? Does it taste good? You might be surprised at what you discover when you really focus on your food.

Try to please yourself in all aspects of your eating. Please yourself by eating delicious foods. Please your whole body, not just your taste buds. Know that you can have whatever you want whenever you want, so you don't have to eat it all now.

REFRAMING VERSUS BINGEING

Please don't misinterpret reframing as permission to binge. You are not reframing if you are bingeing.

- Bingeing means using food as a drug, as a way to numb out. In reframing you practice mindful eating – exactly the opposite of numbing out.

- Bingeing is an out-of-control compulsion. Reframing is a conscious, purposeful choice.

- Bingeing means eating so quickly that you are barely aware of what you are eating before it hits your stomach, and then feeling like crap afterwards. Reframing means enjoying what you eat, savoring every bite, and feeling good about what you're doing.

- Bingeing is a miserable experience that leaves you feeling trapped and ashamed. Reframing is a joyful, freeing experience that is born out of self-respect.

- Bingeing is about self-abuse, self-punishment, and feeling bad. Reframing is about honoring your desires, pleasing yourself, and feeling good.

EATING IS NOT REQUIRED

You do not need to actually eat a food to know that you have the right to eat it. You don't, for example, "reframe chocolate" by eating chocolate. In fact, there is no such thing as "reframing chocolate" or any food. Reframing is not a process of deactivating the power of specific foods, one by one, by eating them! The power is not in the food, it's in you.

Stage 1 is not something you eat your way through; it's something you think your way through. Knowing you have the right to eat junk food does not require you to eat junk food. If a food makes you feel unwell, don't eat it. Having a right means you have a choice. You can eat formerly forbidden foods if you like, or you can choose not to.

Just as you can know you have the right to eat something without actually eating it, you can eat something without feeling you have the right. That serves no purpose, either. Reframing is not about eating different foods; it's about changing how you think.

GAINING WEIGHT IN STAGE 1

People starting Normal Eating right after coming off a diet will tend to regain any weight they lost on the diet, but they would anyway, with or without Normal Eating. There is no reason to gain weight during the Reframing stage other- wise. But there are two errors you can make that will lead to weight gain:

- **You are not fully committed to Normal Eating.** If, in the back of your mind, you are thinking that if Normal Eating doesn't work you will go back to dieting, then the deprivation mindset will never go away. You will never truly believe that your free access to food is permanent, so you'll tend to eat more than usual to "get while the getting is good". Normal Eating requires a change in thinking that can't be faked.

- **You stay stuck in Stage 1.** Some people get the wrong idea that their compulsive eating should stop before they move onto Stage 2. This is not the goal of Stage 1. Reframing will address any feelings of guilt or deprivation you have about certain foods, but these are not the only reasons for emotional eating, or even the main reasons. The emotional work in Stages 2 and 3 is what removes the compulsion. So don't make the very serious error of waiting for cravings to disappear before moving onto Stage 2. If you do this, you will gain weight without end (see the section on "Overcoming Overeating").

Stage 1 is meant to be brief, usually a few weeks at most. You don't have to be 100% perfectly guilt-free to move onto Stage 2. As soon as you can observe your eating without excessive distress, you should move on. Some people move on almost immediately.

WEIGHING YOURSELF

Another question that comes up is weighing yourself.

Have you ever gotten on the scale, seen a two pound gain, and felt suddenly grotesque and enormous when just 10 seconds ago you felt fine? Weirder yet, have you ever noticed that feeling fat makes you want to eat? It's ironic, but that's how emotional eaters deal with pain and distress.

Feeling fat has little to do with your actual body size. You can feel thin one day and fat the next, with a difference in weight of only two pounds – or no pounds. Many people who have lost weight down to their normal size or smaller still feel fat. When you say, "I feel fat", what you're really saying is, "I don't feel good about myself."

Most people who struggle with their weight weigh themselves frequently, often many times a day. Did you ever stop to wonder what you're really looking for from the scale, what's driving the obsession with your weight? The problem is you've come to believe that your weight reflects your value as a human being, and you need to know whether you're okay. It's not unlike constantly asking a lover for reassurance that you're loved. You've put the power to determine your worth outside yourself.

Some people try to deal with obsessive weighing by limiting the frequency. But this doesn't address the core problem, and usually doesn't diminish the obsession, either. You just spend the time between weighings wondering what you weigh. Putting yourself on a "weighing diet" actually can increase the obsession. Nor does throwing out your scale solve anything. That just implies that the number on the scale has so much power you're scared to look at it.

The real solution is to stop giving a mechanical device the power to tell you whether you're okay. Your value as a human being is not contained in a number on a scale! Once you understand that, you can weigh yourself or not, and it's no big deal either way.

TRUSTING YOURSELF

Normal Eating can feel frightening at first. Suddenly there are no rules. You're responsible for your own food choices, and you're not sure you can be trusted. You may fear that Normal Eating can't work for you, that you don't have the ability to choose well.

These doubts come from years of being told that you're not competent to choose your own food, and you'll be dangerously out of control without an externally-defined diet. But it's not true. You *can* do this!

Learning to trust yourself is a core element of Normal Eating, and I'm not just talking about eating choices. We are integrated beings. Either we trust ourselves, or we don't. If you distrust yourself in one area, you will tend to distrust yourself in all areas – food, relationships, money, or whatever.

Happily, the spillover effect goes both ways. As you develop self-trust around food, you will trust yourself more in other areas. With self-trust comes self-respect; you can't trust yourself if you don't respect yourself. Self-respect is the foundation of self-love. Just as you can't love a partner you don't respect (loss of respect means the end of a relationship), you can't love yourself without respecting yourself. When you love yourself, you'll take care of yourself. And when your needs are met, you won't need to self-soothe with food.

It all starts with trusting yourself!

Health Restrictions

People with health issues affected by diet can find Stage 1 especially challenging. If you have diabetes, for example, and can't safely eat sweets, how do you avoid feelings of restriction?

Attitude is everything. You have to view foregoing harmful foods as an act of self-love, a gift to yourself of health and well-being, which, in fact, it is. This is hard to do in Stage 1 when you're still in the grip of compulsion, but you can do it if you think it through. A child whose mother won't let her have a cookie might have a tantrum because she doesn't understand the reason. But you understand the reason, so there's nothing to resent or rebel against. The restriction isn't imposed on you arbitrarily from the outside. It's your choice, and it's a reasonable choice to make. After all, what do you want more, a stupid cookie or your health?

Even with food restrictions, there are countless delicious things to eat. Focus on what you *can* eat, rather than on what you cannot. Buy a specialty cookbook and learn new recipes.

Finally, don't take a black-and-white attitude towards the restriction. If you're not supposed to eat sugar and you eat one cookie, don't then decide that you may as well eat the whole box. Avoiding harmful foods 90% of the time is better than not avoiding them at all.

Stage 2:
Reconnecting

Emotional eaters tend to ignore all aspects of their eating experience except taste. Many people starting on this journey aren't even sure when they're hungry. Partly this is because they haven't let themselves get physically hungry for years, and partly it's because they confuse emotional hunger and physical hunger.

To eat normally, you must be able to differentiate between emotional and physical hunger, know how your body feels after eating different foods, and recognize satiation – the point at which eating one more bite will make you uncomfortable. Before you can eat mainly when hungry, you must be able to identify true hunger!

The goal of Stage 2 is **reconnecting with yourself**, in particular all aspects of your eating experience – both emotional and physical. Reconnecting with physical cues is necessary to turn on your natural, internal controls. Reconnecting with yourself emotionally – becoming able to identify what's bothering you – is necessary for the work you'll do in Stage 3 on learning alternative ways to cope.

Stage 2 is not when you try to eat mainly when hungry – that's Stage 3. In Stage 2 you're just reconnecting with all aspects of your inner experience. Trying to do this and at the same time eat mainly when hungry is too much at once. For now, it's enough to just notice when your desire to eat is emotionally based, and to identify what's triggering it.

The process you go through in Stage 2 is analogous to what happens when you learn to drive a car. At first all the things you have to pay attention to seem like too much at once. But over time, it becomes automatic and effortless. Eventually you'll know how different foods make your body feel as well as how they taste, and you'll easily differentiate between emotional and physical hunger. That's when you're ready to move to Stage 3.

THE EATING EXPERIENCE LOG

The tool you'll use to reconnect with yourself is the Eating Experience Log, which will guide you through careful observation of your physical and emotional reactions. The prerequisite for Stage 2 is the ability to observe your eating without judging it – the goal of Stage 1. Most people keep the log for several months.

The purpose of the log is not to control your eating in any way, but to observe how different ways of eating make you feel. You may still overeat, and you need to be able to observe this without judging too much. If keeping the log triggers self-loathing, you're not ready for Stage 2; work on reframing a bit longer. But if you just feel an occasional twinge of discomfort when logging, that's okay – just remind yourself that you have the right to eat whatever you want.

Feel free to adapt the Eating Experience Log to your own needs. You might, for example, want to log urges to eat, whether or not you act on them. To identify foods that trigger your migraines, log your migraines. If you suspect you have a sensitivity to wheat or dairy, you know what to add to the log!

If you struggle with bulimia, log those urges and actions as well. If you tend to restrict (anorexia), log impulses to starve.

And without question, if you suffer from either anorexia or bulimia, please seek professional help because these are life-threatening conditions. If your medical professional says it's okay to use the Normal Eating program, then go ahead. But if, for instance, part of your treatment for anorexia is to eat on a schedule, whether or not you feel hungry, then you must do this. Normal Eating is not a substitute for professional treatment of these life-threatening conditions.

You can use a small notebook to keep the Eating Experience Log, or you can post your log online in the Normal Eating Support Group (personal blogs area).

LOGGING BEFORE YOU EAT

Before you put food in your mouth – it's very important to do this *before* eating – write down the answers to these questions. The sections that follow explain the purpose of each question and what to look for.

Before Eating
- Date/time
- Thoughts and feelings before eating
- Hunger level to start (use scale)

THOUGHTS AND FEELINGS

The question about thoughts and feelings is to help you connect emotional triggers with the desire to eat. Sometimes triggers are reminders of deep issues from the past (for example, childhood sexual abuse). Sometimes they're uncomplicated, like needing to unwind and give yourself a treat after a day working or caring for others. Sometimes they're related to acute problems in your current life that are uncomfortable to face.

But if you just ask yourself, "What am I feeling?" the answer may be "Nothing." Here's how to get around that.

Try to approach logging in the same way you approached your weight history – gather the facts first. Write down what happened around you in the moment before the thought of eating popped into your head. What was said, what was done, what was happening in your immediate environment?

Here's an example of an important insight I had while logging. In my former job, I was editor of a column in a magazine. The job paid well, but was very demanding. The nature of the column made it difficult to keep up with the relentless, every-two-weeks pace.

One day while working on a column that was a few days late, I received an email message from the executive editor asking where my column was (and not asking very nicely, either). Without thinking – like a robot – I immediately rose from my chair and headed towards the kitchen. I got about halfway there before I thought to ask myself, "Are you hungry?" The answer was no, so instead of continuing into the kitchen, I sat on the couch and asked myself what was going on.

It look less than a minute for me to realize that it was the email from the editor that had triggered the urge to eat. As I continued to sit and think, I became fully aware, for the first time, of how trapped and oppressed my job made me feel. I'd been doing this job for 10 years, and I was burned out to the point of desperation. This was not a comfortable insight because I didn't have any obvious alternatives for employment, but just the awareness caused my urge to eat to evaporate.

I was able to discover the trigger because I checked in with myself in real time. If I'd gotten a snack and then logged about it later, I would never have had the insight.

Your weight history also can offer clues. If you learned, for example, that feeling trapped in a bad situation is a trigger for you, ask yourself if something is making you feel trapped.

RATING YOUR HUNGER

Rate your hunger level using this scale:

Hunger/Satiation Scale

0 - Weak with hunger, running on adrenaline.

1 - Too hungry to care what you eat.

2 - Seriously hungry, must eat now!

3 - Moderately hungry, could wait longer.

4 - Slightly hungry, first thoughts of food.

5 - Neutral, can't feel food in stomach.

6 - Satisfied, feel the food but no discomfort.

7 - Slightly uncomfortable, food pressing a little.

8 - Uncomfortable, stomach painfully distended.

9 - Very overfull, so full you want to lie down.

10 - Stuffed, so full it hurts.

Don't be surprised if at first you have no idea what level you're at. That's very common, and it just shows how badly you need to reconnect. Here's a quote about this from a Normal Eating Support Group member:

> I've only been logging for 3 days but I do get really confused with the numbers. My body feels so wacked out (I'm just coming out of a few years of really strange/ unhealthy diets)... I swear I don't even know hunger from fullness. I thought I was a 4 when I ate dinner tonight... and then I thought I was a 7... then 5 minutes later I thought I was hungry. Then a few minutes later my stomach felt sick and very full. What is this??? It's driving me nuts. I feel like the numbers I write down are so arbitrary - like I'm just guessing.

Over time, as you practice looking inward, you *will* reconnect with your inner cues. Here's a quote from another Normal Eating Support Group member:

> Honestly - when I first started this I thought I would never get it. I didn't think my body would ever speak to me again - after all I put it through... But lo and behold... I am getting messages. The hard part is interpreting what it's saying. It's like being an infant - "What do you want? Are you hungry? Tired? Need a nap? Want your blankie?"

Some general guidelines for recognizing true physical hunger:

- Being hungry is like being in love. If you're not sure, then you're not. When you are, there's no question about it.

- If hunger comes on very suddenly — one minute you're fine, and the next you feel ravenous — then you're experiencing emotional hunger. Physical hunger comes on gradually.

- A growling stomach doesn't necessarily mean hunger, though it can. Growling is caused by activity in your digestive tract that also occurs after eating, it's just louder when your stomach is empty. You can feel hungry without a growling stomach (drinking water will quiet it), and your stomach can growl when you're not hungry.

- Thinking about eating can make you feel hungry. There's no way to avoid thinking about eating at this stage, but it's worth noting this.

You can trust your body to tell you when it needs food. There is no rule that hunger has to come every five hours, or whatever. If you've been regularly overeating for some time, you may feel very little hunger when you first start paying attention to this. Your body senses that it has a surfeit of fuel, and reduces natural hunger in an effort to restore the body to its natural weight. I've noticed this on a small scale, as well. If I've overeaten while on vacation or at holiday time, I'll want very little food for several days afterwards.

Don't worry that your hunger signal will never come. If you don't eat for long enough, you will get hungry and you will know it.

HOW TRUE HUNGER FEELS

Here's how I experience hunger. I'll be absorbed in something else – sitting in front of the computer, maybe – and the thought will occur to me that I'm hungry. Usually my first thought will be that I can't be bothered with that, and I'll return to what I was doing. Then a little while later, the thought will again jump into my head that I'm hungry. Maybe I'll ignore it then, too. Over time, the thought "I'm hungry" starts to jump into my head so frequently that it's intrusive and I can't concentrate anymore. That's when I surrender and go eat.

When you're truly hungry, the only thing that interests you is eating. If you sit down to a meal and you're hungry, you have no interest in reading that book you brought with you to the table, or watching a TV show, or even talking to your meal companions. Have you ever noticed when you're out to dinner with friends, that everyone quiets down when the food first arrives and focuses on their plates? When you're hungry, food is more fascinating than anything else in your environment.

Eating when you're truly hungry is very enjoyable. The French have a saying that hunger is the best condiment, and it's true. When you're hungry, your taste buds are sensitized and everything tastes better.

You know when you've had enough when the food is not so fascinating anymore. When you pause in taking bites to open the book you brought to the table, you're done eating! The food is no longer enough to hold your interest – you need some other entertainment.

Another way to know you've had enough is that the taste of the food is less intense. What started off as delectable no longer tastes as pleasurable. Dulled taste is a key satiation cue, but it's subtle. That's why mindful eating is so important. If you're not paying attention, you'll miss it.

ALWAYS PAUSE BEFORE EATING

If you're in a situation where you can't pull out your logging notebook and write, then at least pause for a moment before eating, perhaps with your eyes closed, and check in with yourself. What are your thoughts and feelings, what's happening around you? What is your hunger level?

Pausing before eating, even if you don't write, will give you useful information. Not pausing, and then writing later from memory, serves no useful purpose. For one thing, it's only in the moment of discomfort before eating – in the pause – that you can connect with what's triggering a craving. Once you've eaten, the reduction in discomfort and the distraction of the food put you out of touch with the trigger *since that is the purpose of compulsive eating.*

There are also some questions to ask yourself after you're done eating, as you'll see. Again, if you're not in a position to write, then pause for a moment after eating and check in with yourself. Ask yourself the log questions in real time. Filling out the eating log later from memory will not give you useful information. The check-in with yourself has to be in the moment.

Sometimes you can't write, but if you can, you should. Writing out your thoughts forces a more thorough self-examination than simply thinking about the questions for a few moments.

It's not always possible to log your eating, but it ought to be possible at least once in every day. Sometimes people say they don't have time to do it when actually they just don't want to do it.

RESISTANCE TO LOGGING

Almost everybody experiences a resistance to logging. The reason has to do with why people overeat in the first place.

Overeating is a fantastic way to distract yourself from disturbing thoughts, feelings, and problems. Once you get into the mode, you can't think about anything except what you're eating, how you shouldn't be eating it, how fat you are, and the diet you're going to go on tomorrow. This is so absorbing that all other thoughts are pushed from your mind.

Logging forces you to be aware of all aspects of your experience – thoughts, feelings, physical sensations. This is the path to freedom from emotional eating, but full awareness also is exactly what you've overeating to avoid. Logging interferes with the payoff you get from emotional eating, and that makes for powerful resistance.

So expect to wrestle with yourself when you start Stage 2. Your first impulse will be to resist the introspection that comes with logging. But if you make yourself do it anyway, the progress you'll see will overcome your resistance and you'll want to do it.

LOGGING AFTER EATING

So far I've only talked about the first part of the Eating Experience Log, the part you write before eating. There is also a part you write after eating. It has two sections:

Eating Experience
- Food eaten
- Amount (number of fists)
- How enjoyable?
- Ate mindfully?
- Distractions
- Thoughts about stopping

After Eating
- Comfort level at stopping point (use scale)
- How body feels after eating
- Thoughts and feelings after eating

If writing down what you ate makes you feel like you're on a diet, then leave it off. It's just there to encourage you to notice how different foods make you feel.

The reason to log how much you're eating is so you can notice how much food it takes to feel satiated. People who routinely overeat are often stunned at how little food it takes to satiate them physically. It can feel scary because it's so different from what you're used to. Noting the amount you ate gives you an anchor and a reality check.

The amount of food is estimated in "fists" because your stomach, unstretched by food, is about the size of your clenched fist. If you mashed up all the food on your plate into a ball, how big would the ball be compared to your clenched fist (more or less)? Is it one fist? Two fists?

Usually one fist of food will take you to a 5 on the Hunger/ Satiation Scale, but not always. Exercise can make a big difference.

When I lived in Vermont I burned wood for heat, and one winter I procrastinated on stacking my wood, which was piled in the driveway in front of the woodshed. A storm was coming that was expected to dump two feet of snow, and I had to get the wood out of the driveway before it hit. First of all I needed to be able to get at the wood, but also having it there would make it very hard for the driveway to be plowed. I had about 2.5 cords of wood to stack, and I spend the entire day – a solid 8 hours – doing nothing but stacking wood. I was afraid to stop because I was right up against the nor'easter. By the time I finished it was dark outside, and it had already started snowing.

I don't know if you've ever stacked wood before, but it's hard labor — especially when you're doing it fast. Besides being aerobic, you really work the muscles in your arms, legs, and back. When I finally finished and came in to eat, it was like I had a bottomless pit where my stomach used to be — or maybe a hollow leg. I ate the amount I usually ate for dinner, and I was still hungry. So I made more food, and I was still hungry.

I ended up eating two to three times more than usual before I felt satiated. I don't know why my stomach didn't feel stretched out. I didn't feel the least bit overfull or uncomfortable, and usually I'd feel very uncomfortable eating that much food.

So don't worry about the number of fists you're eating. Just follow your hunger.

Try to eat mindfully and note whether you did. If there were distractions that prevented mindful eating, note that, too.

There are many reasons to notice how much you enjoyed the food. One I've already mentioned — enjoyment is greater when you're hungry. Another reason is that enjoyment is greater with mindful eating. Noticing that you enjoy your food the most when you're hungry and eating mindfully makes you to want to eat when hungry and eat mindfully!

The "thoughts about stopping" question is to help you identify satiation cues. People tend to have trouble identifying when they've had enough. Typically people can eat when hungry before they can stop when full. But over time, if you pay attention to your eating experience, you'll learn to identify that "just enough" feeling.

Rate your satiation level when you're done eating using the Hunger/Satiation Scale, and also notice how your body feels in general. Do you feel energized or sluggish? Did your body enjoy that brownie, or did only your taste buds enjoy it? I love the taste of homemade bread, but I've noticed that it gives me heartburn if I eat it later in the day. The memory of the discomfort dissuades me from eating bread in the evening.

Body wisdom makes what's good for you pleasurable so you'll do what's good for you. Reconnecting with every aspect of your eating experience – not just taste – is how you turn on your inner controls. Noticing the pleasure of eating when hungry will make you prefer eating when hungry. Noticing how energized and clear-headed you feel after a healthy meal will make you want to eat healthy meals. But to fully reconnect, you need to experiment.

BE A SCIENTIST, DO EXPERIMENTS

If you always eat similar foods, you may not be able to tell how a food makes your body feel because you have nothing to compare it with. Try pasta for dinner one night, then chicken with veggies the next night, and then cake for dinner the next. All three will satisfy hunger, but they have very different effects on your body. Notice how much

NORMAL EATING FOR NORMAL WEIGHT

better you feel when you eat foods that nourish. If you don't try it, you can't know.

Similarly, if you always eat before you're really hungry, you can't know how hunger heightens taste and pleasure. Try waiting to varying degrees of hunger before eating. At what hunger level does food taste the best? Do you notice that if you let yourself get too hungry (below a 2), you will tend to overeat?

To learn what satiation feels like (being "just satisfied" versus overfull), try eating to different levels of fullness and compare how your body feels. Does it take longer before you're hungry again if you eat more?

See if it's true that eating breakfast is good for you, even if you're not hungry when you first get up. If it's really true that energy is low and thinking impaired when you don't eat breakfast, wouldn't you notice that? Try it both ways and see how you feel.

Also, don't forget thirst. Sometimes when you think you're hungry, you're really thirsty. See if you can tell the difference.

Note that you can trust your thirst to tell you when to drink water, just as you can trust your hunger to tell you when to eat. You don't need drinking rules such as eight glasses of water per day any more than you need eating rules. You can trust your body to tell you what it needs.

Have fun with this; try things. I don't mean just try junk food, but also try healthy food. Try a range of eating experiences so you can compare how your body reacts.

THE WHISPER OF BODY WISDOM

Most of all, try to listen to the whisper of body wisdom – to what your body wants you to eat. I've talked a lot about hunger and satiation cues, but those are not the only messages that body wisdom sends. Your body also will tell you when it's not getting enough Vitamin A by making you want to eat carrots. It will tell you when you're not getting enough roughage by making you want a salad. These urges are subtle – body wisdom speaks in a whisper. They're not cravings so much as a "taste" for something. You may not be able to tell the two apart at first, but eventually you will.

When you're hungry and you feel more like eating one type of food than another, it's because the food you're attracted to provides something your body needs nutritionally. That's how animals in the wild manage to eat a perfectly balanced diet without any nutritionists advising them. It's inborn body wisdom, and we humans have it, too.

So work on reconnecting with all aspects of body wisdom, not just hunger and satiation. Eventually this will lead you to want to eat a healthy diet simply because you feel so much better when you do.

❧ ❧

GRAZING & FEAR OF HUNGER

Not all emotional eating is bingeing and eating past full. Some people "graze" – eating only a little at a time, but very frequently. Grazers may never feel overly full, but they never experience true physical hunger, either.

Emotional eaters frequently fear the experience of hunger, for reasons I'll talk about shortly, and this could be one reason for grazing. But grazers may not fear hunger so much as feeling "empty".

Food can have a symbolic meaning for people. If you have heavy demands on you, you may see food as a way to fuel yourself to meet these demands – as "emotional fuel" rather than a physical fuel. If you're empty you have nothing to give. You can't "run on empty". If you find yourself grazing when you have a difficult task to do, maybe it's not simple procrastination – maybe you're trying to fuel yourself to do it.

On the other hand, if you do a lot of preventative eating – eating before going out so you don't get hungry – then fear of hunger probably plays a role.

EATING TO FEEL SAFE

Virtually all emotional eaters have a fear of hunger, though they may not realize it since they often haven't experienced true physical hunger for years. This frequently comes up for the first time in Stage 2, when people try to wait for hunger before eating.

Eating and satiation are deeply associated with safety and contentment because it was ingrained in us as infants. We were hungry, we were helpless to do anything about it, and we were terrified as well as physically uncomfortable. We howled. Someone came and fed us. What relief! And forevermore, eating and satiation are associated with comfort and safety.

Feeling hungry can evoke a wordless fear from infancy, or unpleasant memories of being sent to bed without dinner for misbehaving. (It's a very bad idea for parents to use food as reward or punishment.)

This fear does go away. I no longer experience it, and I used to experience it strongly. I'd eat before I went out for a few hours, even though I wasn't hungry, for fear I'd get hungry and not have access to food. I no longer need to do that, or even think about doing that. I think it's because I've gotten to know my hunger cues well enough that I know when eating in two hours will be fine, and when I need to arrange for food.

EATING OUT OF BOREDOM

A lot of people say they eat out of boredom. You may have said it yourself. But boredom is a tricky thing; it almost always masks something else. Here's an example posted in the Normal Eating Support Group:

> If my boyfriend is in the house, I can entertain myself endlessly with books and chores and hobbies and walks and all the stuff I like to do. But when he's out for the evening, those things just bore the heck out of me and eating is sometimes the only thing that will entertain me. Hmmmm. I think I am confusing "bored" with "lonely"!
>
> LOL. I am such a supersleuth!

The only time a person can be legitimately and purely bored is when they are trapped in a situation where they are physically prevented from leaving or doing something to stimulate and entertain themselves. One of the most boring experiences of my life was a required class in my first year of graduate school, co-taught by a pair of aging professors who we nicknamed the "Sominex Twins". It was desperately, mind-numbingly boring, but there was no escape. I couldn't leave, and because it was a small class where everyone sat around a table, I couldn't do something to divert myself without attracting attention. I also couldn't chance spacing out and then being called on and having no idea what was going on. That is boredom.

True boredom requires being trapped. If you are free to do something to entertain yourself and you're not doing it, the problem isn't boredom. The problem is that you're not doing something interesting and fun when you could be, and the question you need to ask yourself is why.

You can think you're trapped when you're not — for example, feeling stuck in a boring job. People usually have many more options than they realize or acknowledge. Often taking action is difficult, but then the problem is not the boring job; the problem is reluctance to take a scary and difficult action.

Sometimes what people call "boredom" is anxiety from lack of distraction. When you're trying to avoid thinking about something that makes you anxious, it's good to have a lot of busy-ness around you. During quiet times — for example, lulls on the job, or when first getting into bed at night — these disturbing thoughts start to break into consciousness. Eating at quiet times is often described as "eating out of boredom", but actually it's eating to distract from disturbing thoughts that threaten to break into consciousness.

If you think that the main reason you eat is because you're bored, you probably need to look a little further and ask yourself some questions. Why are you bored? Are you trapped in a class with the Sominex Twins, or serving on a jury in a mind-numbingly dull trial? Or is there something you could do to entertain yourself, but you're not doing it?

If it's the latter, then you need to ask yourself why you're doing nothing when you could be doing something. Why are you watching television when you could be learning something on the internet or reading a mind-broadening book? Why are you staying at a boring job instead of taking steps to find a new one?

If it's quiet time that's triggering you, then you need to allow the scary thoughts and feelings to surface. They are always scarier when you are trying to avoid them.

Wasting Food

A common sticking point when trying not to eat past full is the deeply ingrained idea that you must "clean your plate".

This could come from parental injunctions in childhood: "If you took it, you must eat it." "You can't have dessert until you clean your plate." "Oh, you ate all your dinner – what a good girl!" If it's just an old habit, a useful exercise is to leave one bite of food on your plate at each meal, just to get used to the idea.

But I don't think that old parental injunctions fully explain this. It can be amazingly hard to stop eating when there's still food on your plate, even if you know you're no longer hungry. You almost feel obligated to eat it all, as if it's a job you've been given.

I believe this is a self-esteem issue – a question of what you feel entitled to do, how you rank your comfort compared to other considerations. You need to have the conviction that your desires, needs, and comfort matter more than any other considerations about wasted food. Then you'll feel entitled to throw away food, to eat according to hunger rather than what happens to be on your plate. This requires a certain amount of self-esteem.

If you're hung up on the idea that it's wrong to waste food, remember two things:

- Anything can be wrapped and eaten later.

- Food dumped down your throat when you're not hungry is still wasted – it's just going through you first. Don't treat your body like a garbage pail.

Finally, if you're tempted to keep eating just because the food tastes good, remind yourself that deprivation is a thing of the past. You're free to eat whatever you want whenever you want. You can have this food at any time. So why make yourself uncomfortable now by overeating?

STAGE 3: RELEARNING

In Stage 2 you learn to reconnect with your internal cues. It's confusing at first, but eventually you can easily distinguish between physical and emotional hunger, you know when you're hungry and when you've had enough (even if you keep eating), and you can hear the whisper of body wisdom (even if you don't act in accordance with it). That's when you're ready to move on to Stage 3.

In Stage 2 you learned to pause before eating. In Stage 3 you'll turn the "pause" into a "stop". You will have met the goal of Stage 3 when 90% or more of your eating is for hunger, and cravings are essentially gone (or a rare occurrence). Stage 2 is about observing your behavior; Stage 3 is about changing it.

To eat when hungry and stop when full, you must **relearn how you deal with stress**. As I said in the chapter on "Compulsive Eating", non-hunger eating serves two main functions:

- To distract from what's really bothering you.
- To soothe the pain of unmet needs.

So in Stage 3 you will learn to uncover what's really bothering you, and take action to meet your true need. This is not comfortable or easy, but you have the skills to do it from your work in Stages 1 and 2.

Relearning is the hardest stage of Normal Eating, and generally takes people the longest – usually about a year.

EXPECT DISCOMFORT

Emotional eaters convert almost all uncomfortable feelings into cravings for food. That's the emotional habit you need to break. When you're able to recognize your feelings and needs in real time, you'll no longer experience the compulsion to eat.

So when you have a craving – every time you have a craving – you must sit with the discomfort long enough to figure out what's really bothering you. This will ultimately remove the compulsion and give you real relief, but first you have to endure the discomfort of sitting with cravings.

There is no way to stop emotional eating without discomfort. Expect it – brace yourself for it.

If you think that if you analyze your feelings enough, you will be able to stop emotional eating without discomfort, you are mistaken. No amount of analysis can remove cravings, or the discomfort of not acting on cravings. Armchair analysis of why you eat, such as Geneen Roth recommends in *Why Weight?*, is ineffective and can keep you stuck. It gives you an illusion of working on the problem when actually you're not. You can't think your way out of emotional eating, and trying just leads to analysis paralysis.

Also don't fall into the most insidious trap of all: telling yourself that you can't stop emotional eating right now because you have problems in your life. First of all, everybody always has problems, so you can use this as an excuse forever. Second, the whole point is to learn better ways to deal with your problems since emotional eating is escapist and ineffective. And third, this attitude implies that if you didn't have problems, you could stop emotional eating without effort or discomfort, and that is untrue. There is no way around the effort and discomfort.

To stop emotional eating, you must be willing to tolerate some discomfort — it's that simple. That's not what someone with an addictive personality wants to hear (see the chapter on "The Nature of Addiction"), but that is the fact. *Sometimes in life, you just have to feel bad.*

Change comes in this order: First your actions change, then your thinking changes, and then — last — your feelings change. The discomfort of sitting with cravings will only go away after you stop acting on the cravings. That's because it's only when you stop acting on the cravings that the cravings disappear.

Think It Through

When you're sitting with a craving, there are some things you can say to yourself that will help. First, simply acknowledge the craving. Just say to yourself, "Hmm, I notice I have an urge to eat though I'm not hungry. I wonder what that's about." This detaches you from the urge, puts you in the role of observer, and reinforces that an urge is just a feeling and doesn't mandate action. You can choose not to act on an urge.

It also helps to remind yourself that whatever is making you want to eat will not be fixed by eating. If you have a difficult life problem and you eat to numb out, you'll make yourself feel temporarily better without taking any constructive action. Afterwards, you'll still have the same problem, plus additional problems stemming from compulsive eating (feeling bad about yourself, physical discomfort, health problems, etc.). The only problem that eating can fix is hunger.

Plus there's a big payoff if you stick with this. If you don't give yourself the artificial "out" of numbing your feelings with food, then the only way to feel better is to address the underlying problem. If you give up food as a crutch, you'll start facing and fixing problems you've been evading for years. Your whole life will get better.

FIND THE TRIGGER

To address the underlying problem, you first need to figure out what it is. This can be tricky because the purpose of compulsive eating is to distract from the real problem. To identify the trigger, you must avoid distractions (including, of course, acting on the urge to eat!). Don't turn on the television or call someone. Sit quietly and allow your feelings to bubble up. You may want to close your eyes to look inward, or write in a journal.

Think about the events that immediately preceded the urge to eat, no matter how small – a phone call, a door knock, a comment, a paragraph you read, a passing thought. What was happening just before the impulse came into your head? Let your mind play over these things, and see where your thoughts take you. Often that's all that's necessary. I gave an example from my own life in the chapter on Stage 2 (see the section on "Thoughts and Feelings"). Here's an example from a Normal Eating Support Group member:

> I was logging yesterday and in the afternoon was really hit with the need to numb out and just eat and eat... sat with my feelings instead and guess what – they surfaced! I realized that I had been more anxious and sad about my daughter moving out next month than I was acknowledging.
>
> She is 22 and just finished college. She stayed at home and went to a local college and just graduated in May. She is moving out in August and going to graduate school. I was surprised at my feelings because I am ready for her to move on, feel like I have done a good job

raising her. I have made a point to let her go emotionally and gradually ever since high school started, so I felt like I was ready.

I think the feelings are not so much sadness at seeing her go, but anxiety that I now have permission to do more things in life, become someone besides her mom – a big piece of my identity is going out the door as well. This really surprised me, because I have always made a point not to have her be the total focus of my life – I have hobbies and other interests, spend time away with my husband, etc.

Now I have some emotions to look at and work through. I honestly would never have realized this if I had started eating.

Sometimes you have to dig a little to find the real issue. For example, let's say you had an argument with your partner, and then wanted to eat. You know the argument triggered the craving, but that doesn't tell you what unmet need you're looking to soothe with food. Maybe you're worried that your anger means you're not a nice person. In that case, what you need is self-acceptance. Maybe you feel disrespected by your partner, and what you need is to stand up for yourself. Or maybe you feel frightened, or lonely. Just knowing that the urge is related to the argument is not enough.

The weight history you wrote in Stage 1 can provide clues. If you noticed, for example, that you tend to eat when you feel rejected, you can ask yourself if you're feeling rejected. Directed questions may yield more insight than simply asking yourself what's wrong.

It's not enough to know you're unhappy; you need to know what's causing the unhappiness. Unhappiness signals unmet needs. If you know what those needs are, then you can take action to address them. If you just know you're unhappy, then the only way to feel better is some sort of comfort behavior like eating.

The goal in Stage 3 is not to find alternative comfort behaviors. The goal is to identify and address your unmet needs. When you have a constant headache from banging your head against a wall, the solution isn't more aspirin – it's to stop banging your head against the wall.

TAKE AN ACTION

Sometimes just allowing yourself to become fully aware of what's bothering you is enough to eliminate the compulsion to eat. But if you're soothing the pain of unmet needs, you'll need to take action to address the problem. The action you take doesn't have to completely solve the problem – most times it won't – but it should directly address the problem and move you incrementally towards a solution.

Many problems in life don't have easy solutions or perfect solutions, and people can feel so hopeless that they don't see their options. But there is always something you can do to make a situation better or easier. Small acts of self-care and self-assertion can make a world of difference in how you feel. So can changing your self-talk. Even a small action removes the feeling of helplessness that so often triggers emotional eating.

You don't have to solve all your problems for compulsive eating urges to go away. You just have to allow awareness of the problems to fully surface, and start to take steps towards solving them.

The problems that people eat over can range from simple to traumatic. Often people eat in the evening after a long day of work. If this is your pattern, then you may simply need to relax and do something that feels good. In that case, a comfort activity like a warm bath could be an effective action. But if you're eating in the evening because you feel lonely coming home to an empty house, or you're mad at your husband for not helping with children and dinner, then a warm bath is not going to fix the problem. Nor will a warm bath help if you're unhappy in your job. You don't have to up and quit, but you can at least look through job listings. If you have no time to yourself, you can work on ways to make time. What's important is that the action address the unmet need. It has to do more than just soothe.

BE PATIENT

You probably won't be able to do this the first time you try. Or if you're successful the first time, you may fail the second time. As I said at the start of this chapter, it usually takes at least a year to achieve the goals of Stage 3. Sometimes you won't be able to figure out what's bothering you. Sometimes sitting with the craving will bring up unbearable anxiety and you'll give in to it. But if you continue to try in a consistent and honest way, your ability to decode and deactivate cravings will continue to improve. Ultimately, the cravings will go away completely.

What you don't ever want to do is say this to yourself:

> "X terrible thing happened to me today, so I binged. Oh well. When my life isn't difficult anymore, then I'll be able to eat normally."

Instead, say this:

> "X terrible thing happened to me today. I sat with the feelings for as long as I could, but I couldn't find another way to cope and ended up eating. Still, I credit myself for pausing as long as I did, and next time I'll try again."

Emotional eating is never a viable alternative or a good way to deal with stress. You may not be able to stop doing it yet, but you should never rationalize the behavior as okay. *You* are okay, but the behavior is not okay because it's harmful to you. It's not good self-care.

It's important that you be able to condemn the behavior without condemning yourself. That allows you to eventually stop being self-destructive. If you condemn yourself, you'll just be more self-destructive. If you fail to label self-destructive behavior as undesirable, you'll stay stuck – that's self-indulgence, not self-acceptance. Forgive yourself if you give in to emotional eating, but don't ever tell yourself that it's an okay thing to do. (For more on this, see the section on self-acceptance in the chapter "How to Love Yourself".)

One last note... If you're in a miserable or dangerous situation that you don't know how to get out of on your own, or if the feelings you're suppressing with food are rooted in deep childhood trauma, please seek professional help. Normal Eating is not a substitute for a licensed therapist.

STAGE 4: CHOOSING

In Stage 3 you learned to stop using food as an emotional crutch. It's a difficult habit to break, but once you do, you are free from compulsive urges to eat. When 90% or more of your eating is for hunger and cravings are mostly a thing of the past, you're finally able to **choose what you eat**. Stage 4 is about learning to make good food choices.

Since the purpose of eating is to nourish the body, that means eating in ways that promote health. Some people are disappointed that Normal Eating ultimately involves a voluntary transition to a healthy diet. They hope that as long as they eat only when hungry, they can continue make choices based on emotional craving rather than physical need. I've even had people get angry at me and tell me I've tricked them – that I start off saying they can eat whatever they want, and end up preaching about nutrition. But Stage 4 is not the secret Normal Eating diet sprung on you at the end.

If you are fully reconnected with your body's inner wisdom and not driven by emotional compulsion, you will want to eat a healthy diet. Body wisdom is not limited to hunger and satiation cues. It gives you a taste for whatever foods meet your current nutritional needs, and then rewards you by making you feel terrific.

HAZARDS OF PROCESSED FOOD

There's a problem, however, and it's a serious one. Our modern world has invented edible substances (I hesitate to call them foods) that turn the natural instincts of body wisdom against us. Animals in the wild never get fat. Domesticated dogs and cats do. That's because domesticated animals don't eat their natural diet. They eat edible substances invented in labs – packaged, processed pet foods. The more processed food you eat, the less you can rely on body wisdom for food choices because processed foods trick our bodies. That's why it's important to supplement body wisdom with information about nutrition.

Learning about nutrition doesn't wipe out your ability to listen to your body. What drowns out body wisdom is compulsion. Body wisdom speaks in a whisper. Intellectual knowledge speaks quietly, and listens as well as speaks. Compulsion screams so loudly that you can't hear anything else. You don't have to turn off your brain to eat normally, just your compulsion!

In Stage 4, you learn self-care with regard to food, how to make choices for yourself in much the same way that a parent monitors the diet of a child. You want to make sure that you get what you need nutritionally without being completely rigid about it. You may occasionally eat foods without nutritional value just because they taste good, but mostly you'll eat to nourish your body.

You learned in Stage 2 that eating just one nutritious meal can make you feel good. Eating a nutritionally dense diet over time can transform your whole experience of life. How could it be otherwise? We are flesh and blood beings, and not just below the neck. Our brains are flesh and blood, too. Your muscles, your brain chemistry – every part of you – is manufactured from the food you eat. If you don't provide your body with adequate nutrition, you will pay the price in both body and mind.

THE NATURAL HUMAN DIET

There's a lot of debate about what constitutes good nutrition. It's clarifying to take the long view. What did we evolve eating? What is the natural human diet?

We are *Homo sapiens*; that's the name of our species. "Homo", latin for human, is our genus. Human beings – the homo genus – first appeared on Earth about 2.6 million years ago, signaling the start of the Paleolithic Era. From that time until just 10,000 years ago – more than 2 million years – all humans lived in hunter-gatherer societies. They ate the plants they found growing in the wild – fruits, roots, leaves, nuts. They ate little or no grain (the seeds of plants in the grass family) because grain seeds are tiny and difficult to gather, and also require cooking to remove toxicity. They ate the meat of animals they hunted – mammals (herbivores), birds, and fish. They ate eggs only rarely (birds only lay eggs in spring). On rare occasion they'd eat honey, but they had to brave bees to get it. The only milk product they ate was mother's milk for the first few years of life, and never again after they were weaned. You can't get milk from a wild animal – they don't stand still for that.

This was the Paleolithic diet. Since it's what we evolved eating, it's arguably the healthiest way to eat. But it's also very expensive (only fresh foods, no cheap grains), and it's difficult to eat so differently from the public at large. I know because I tried it. I never realized how much of the Western diet revolves around grain and milk until I tried to stop eating them. My body felt great when I was eating this way, but the cost and inconvenience were ultimately too much for me.

The human diet changed drastically about 10,000 years ago with the Neolithic Revolution, when people began farming and raising animals for food rather than hunting and gathering. It was at this time that foods made from grain and the milk of other animals first appeared in the human diet. 10,000 years is not very long to adapt to such a drastic shift, so many people have problems digesting grain and milk products. Even if you don't have full-blown Celiac

Disease or lactose intolerance, grain and milk can harm health in more subtle ways. This isn't true for everyone; it depends on the individual.

But the change in our diets with the Neolithic Revolution pales in comparison to the change after the Industrial Revolution, particularly after the rise of consumerism and convenience foods in the mid 20th century. And our bodies have had no time at all to adapt. 10,000 years is short in evolutionary terms. 150 years isn't even a blink – it's just a few generations.

Before the Industrial Revolution, what we ate was generally recognizable as something from nature – or at least started off that way in our kitchens. Bread may not look like grain, but if you make it yourself, you see the flour and other ingredients that go into it. When you make your own food, it doesn't contain artificial flavors, chemical preservatives, or anything else not from nature.

When the universe of foods you choose from comes from nature, you can rely on body wisdom alone to guide your choices. But we live in a world filled with lab-created edible substances, specifically engineered to use our body wisdom against us (so we eat more and buy more). Salt and sugar are the food industry's most potent weapons.

SALT, SUGAR, AND FAT

Humans enjoy sweetness because in nature, sweetness is a sign that fruits and vegetables are at their peak of ripeness, and when they're at their peak of ripeness, they're also at their peak nutritionally. The food industry exploits this natural preference by creating refined forms of pure sugar, and adding it to virtually everything. If you read labels on processed foods you will see it. Anything that ends with "-ose" is a sugar (dextrose, fructose, sucrose, etc.).

Large amounts of refined sugar disrupt natural control mechanisms. When you eat something sweet – especially on an empty stomach – the "off" signal never comes. You never feel satiated; you just want to eat more. Any simple carbohydrate has this effect since it's quickly converted to sugar in the body – for example, grain stripped of the germ and bran (refined white flour).

Salt also distorts our hunger and satiation cues. People love salt because it's required for life, but was hard to come by for early humans living inland from the ocean. Those who had a taste for salt and sought it out stayed alive to reproduce; those who didn't take the time to find salt got sick and died. Our bodies crave salt to ensure we make the effort to get it. Today salt is readily available, and the food industry exploits this natural craving by dumping salt – like sugar – into virtually all processed foods. Excess salt in the diet can cause high blood pressure and other problems.

And then there's fat.

Not all fat is bad; just chemically altered fat is bad. Trans fats (chemically altered to make liquid fats solid, like for margarine) have been found to cause cancer. Read labels and avoid anything that contains trans fats.

People have a natural liking for fat because it's energy-dense – that is, it's high in calories for its weight. For most of human evolution, the food supply was unreliable and going hungry was common. A taste for energy-dense food evolved to keep us from starving when food was scarce.

But think about this: there is no food in nature that is high in both fat and sugar. Nuts are high in fat, but not sugar. Fruit and honey are high in sugar, but have no fat. It took modern chemistry to join the two in ice cream and other high fat desserts. Humans are biologically inclined to love a food that's high in both fat and sugar, but the combination totally short-circuits body wisdom. You won't get a signal to stop eating until you're full to the point of discomfort.

So what do you do? You don't have to stop eating anything sweet or salty, but you do need to be aware that when you're eating something unnaturally sweet or salty, you can't rely on body wisdom to tell you when you stop. You must use your brain. Decide in advance how much of it you choose to eat, eat it, and then get it out of your sight because otherwise you'll probably keep eating it.

It helps to avoid eating sugar on an empty stomach. Refined carbohydrates like sugar cause a sharp spike in blood sugar if there's nothing else in your stomach. That can lead to reactive hypoglycemia (your body overcompensates, causing your blood sugar to drop too low), and low blood sugar will make you crave sugar again.

You can avoid the salt trap by simply eating less of it. I eat very little processed food (which is usually very salty), and I don't use much salt when I cook or at the table. You might think that would make everything tasteless, but actually it's just the opposite. When you stop masking the taste of everything with salt, you become able to appreciate subtle flavors and you enjoy your food more. Also, you discover that there is such a thing as too much salt. Many restaurants and delis use so much salt that I can't eat their food.

WHAT IS GOOD NUTRITION?

So with this background, let's return to the question of what constitutes good nutrition. Theories differ, but one general principle is beyond dispute. Fresh unprocessed food, still recognizable as it appeared in nature, is good for your health. An apple, for example, looks the same in your hand as it did on the tree. The less processing the better, since processed foods are loaded with salt, sugar, and artificial ingredients. Some heavily processed foods are marketed as "health foods" – for example, granola bars – but don't you believe it. If it's highly processed, it does not promote health. There are no granola bar trees.

My personal view is that the Paleolithic diet is the gold standard because this is what humans evolved eating – which is not to say I don't eat milk or grain. I do. But I believe that humans are natural omnivores – eating animals as well as vegetables. Vitamin B12, a necessary nutrient, only can be obtained from animal products. Vegetarians, especially vegans, must take it in pill form or suffer anemia.

I respect vegetarianism as a moral choice, but I don't agree with those who say it's the natural human diet.

I also disagree with the advice to eat a low-fat diet. The Paleolithic diet contained plenty of fat. There are certain types of fat (the "essential fatty acids") that are necessary for life and only can be obtained from food. If you don't eat enough fat, you'll be hungry all the time, your hair will be dull, and your skin will be dry. I do stay away from the damaged fats in processed foods ("trans fats"), because they're artificial and carcinogenic.

That said, it's true that the red meat our ancestors ate was lower in fat overall, and the fat it contained was higher in omega-3 fatty acids. That's because the wild animals they ate fed on grass, the natural diet of a grazing animal. Commercially raised cattle are fed grain – not their natural diet. So I buy grass-fed beef. That's easy to do if you're in a rural area. If you're in a city, go to Whole Foods. They carry it.

I also try to eat other foods that are high in omega-3 fatty acids like fish. Grain is high in omega-6 fatty acids, so the prevalence of grain in our diet – including the diet of animals we eat – disturbs the natural ratio of omega-3 to omega-6 fatty acids in the foods we eat. Insufficient omega-3 fatty acids can lead to diseases of inflammation.

It's also worth noting that the reason commercial meat producers feed grain to cattle is because it causes them to gain weight quickly. Grain tends to have the same effect on humans. It also can fatten domestic pets. Cats and dogs are naturally carnivorous, but most commercial pet food contains grain because it's cheap.

The Paleolithic diet was moderately low in carbohydrates, but not extremely low. It generally included plenty of fruits and starchy root vegetables, but no grain. There are exceptions. The traditional diet of the Inuit (Eskimos living near the North Pole) is entirely meat – protein and fat – since vegetables don't grow in the ice. And yet the Inuit thrived. That's because there are essential amino acids (proteins) and essential fatty acids, but there's no such thing as an "essential carbohydrate".

That doesn't mean you have to eat a low-carb diet – I just mention it for information and perspective. I eat toast from homemade bread for breakfast every morning. A low-carb diet causes blood pressure to drop and mine is low to start. When I don't eat enough carbohydrates, my blood pressure drops so low that I feel unwell. If your blood pressure is high, eating fewer carbohydrates may reduce it to normal.

EATING FOR HEALTH VS. SLIMNESS

It's important to note that eating for health is not the same as eating for slimness. Learning the calorie content of different foods is not the same as learning about nutrition. A highly processed Weight Watchers meal may be low in calories, but it's not good for your health. A natural, full-fat food is healthier than a food processed to be unnaturally low in fat using artificial ingredients.

When you eat for health, you achieve a normal weight as a side effect of general health. Eating for slimness rather than health can backfire. People can eat in some very unhealthy ways in pursuit of slimness. Health is beautiful. If you eat in ways that damage your health, you won't look as good – it's as simple as that. Plus you may not even end up slim. When your body doesn't get the nutrition it needs, it can attempt to adapt through slowed metabolism and cravings.

OLD HANG-UPS

If eating for health still seems like a diet, if you can't conceive of choosing it voluntarily and the very thought of a salad gives you dieting flashbacks, you need to work on your thinking. Continually repeating to yourself that eating nourishing food means deprivation will make you resent eating vegetables and prefer cake, regardless of how they make your body feel. Correct irrational thoughts when you catch them running through your head, and tell yourself the truth:

Eating vegetables doesn't mean deprivation. Deprivation is denying your body the nutrition it needs.

If you keep repeating this truth to yourself, you will feel differently about eating vegetables. For more on this, see the chapter on "Thought Stopping".

How to Lose Weight

D id you jump to this chapter before reading anything else? If so, go back and read the first chapter, "Desperately Seeking Slimness", about why it's virtually impossible to lose weight when you care too much about it.

If you've gone through all four stages of Normal Eating and have done the necessary emotional work, then continue reading.

For Stage 4 Eyes Only

If you've been eating normally for a while and your weight isn't moving towards normal, then these are the possibilities:

- You haven't given it enough time. Weight loss through attuned eating tends to be slow.

- Your normal weight is higher than you want it to be – you just naturally carry some fat.

- An unnaturally high proportion of the foods you eat have a high energy-density.

- You're chronically stressed, or eating just a little past full without realizing it.

SLOW LOSS VERSUS NO LOSS

There's a big difference between slow loss and no loss. If you're losing slowly you're doing fine. Weight loss through attuned eating tends to be slow. This may frustrate you, but it has advantages.

- It puts much less stress on your body. Rapid weight loss is so physically stressful that it's been shown to shorten lifespan.

- It gives you time to adapt emotionally to your changing appearance.

- It prevents your body from going into starvation mode, a slow-down in metabolism that makes weight loss all but impossible.

- It tends to be permanent. Weight lost quickly is often regained; weight lost slowly usually stays off.

So be patient. Focus on being comfortable with yourself and your eating, and let your weight take care of itself.

Your Normal Weight?

There is a certain amount of individual variation in what's normal – up to maybe 30 pounds. If you're always trying to lose 10 pounds, you may already be at your normal weight. Some people are naturally small-boned and thin, and some are naturally larger. If being very thin isn't normal for you, then you only can look that way by going hungry. Starving yourself is not a normal or healthy way to eat.

If you were slim when you were younger and weigh more now in middle age, you still may be at your normal weight. People typically weigh 15 pounds more at age 50 than they did at age 20 due to loss of muscle mass and other metabolic changes.

It's not entirely bad. As people age, the layer of fat beneath their skin starts thin. Cheeks hollow out, and skin hangs more on the bones. You lose that ripe, rounded quality of youth. So weighing the same at 50 as you did at 20 can make you look older. You may look better with an extra 15 pounds. Also (and more importantly), women need a little extra fat after menopause to prevent osteoporosis; estrogen is stored in body fat.

Energy-Dense Foods

Are raw and lightly cooked fruits and vegetables a significant and regular part of your diet? If not, that's the problem.

Fresh fruits and vegetables have a low energy-density – that is, they are low in calories by volume – because they're low in fat (with some exceptions), and high in water and soluble fiber (that's the good kind). You can fill up on foods with a low energy-density without eating a lot of calories. Plus you need them for health.

If you eat plenty foods with a low energy-density, you'll have wonderfully functioning bowels and you'll easily maintain your normal weight. If you don't, you'll be constipated and prone to weight gain, even if you eat only when hungry.

Our hunger and satiation cues are calibrated for a diet high in fresh fruits and vegetables since that's what we evolved eating. One of the body's satiation cues is the feeling of food pressing against the walls of your stomach. If all the food you eat has a high energy-density, you'll need to eat too many calories to feel satiated.

Since processed foods tend to have a high energy-density, the modern solution to this problem is to count calories. There's even a new law in New York City requiring fast food restaurants to list the calorie content of menu items. But this is no solution!

The solution is to correct the nutritional profile of the foods you eat. Eat less processed food and more fresh fruits and vegetables!

Eating Past Full

This question from a Normal Eating Support Group member comes up quite a bit:

> What difference does it make how much you eat if you always wait until you are hungry before you eat again?

Overeating was mostly unknown for the first 2 million years of human evolution. It's a phenomenon of the modern age. So eating too much at once can overwhelm the body's ability to give correct feedback.

Your body's hunger and satiation cues will work perfectly if you eat healthy foods and stop before any discomfort (5 or 6 on the Hunger/Satiation Scale). If you eat processed foods with added sugar and salt, you may not get a clear satiation cue. If you then overeat to the point of discomfort (7-10 on the Hunger/Satiation Scale), your body will be doubly confused.

Weight Loss Physiology

There is one more key factor at play. Weight loss is not a straight calculation of calories eaten and energy burned. The physiology of weight loss is complex.

The body tries hard to maintain its weight since both gaining and losing are physically stressful. Though it resists gaining as well as losing, it especially resists losing. This is an evolutionary adaptation to prevent us from starving too easily since our ancestors often went hungry. When your calorie intake drops significantly, your body helpfully slows your metabolism so you can conserve energy and maintain your weight. That's why highly restrictive diets can backfire.

If you have a history of chronic dieting, you may not be losing weight because your metabolism is slowed. Have patience. It takes time to return to normal.

To lose weight, you need to eat just barely what your body needs, no more and no less. If you eat less, your metabolism will slow. If you eat more, your body will maintain its weight or gain. You can't rely on outside rules to tell you how much this is. Only body wisdom can tell you.

I've found that if I wait until I'm at 2 on the Hunger/ Satiation Scale before eating, and stop eating at 5, I will lose weight. But if I eat when I'm at 3 and stop at 6 – a perfectly fine way to eat – I maintain my weight but don't lose. For someone with a faster metabolism than mine, it may be different.

Stress also affects your weight. I'm sure you've heard of the fight-or-flight response. Among other things, acute stress causes digestion to cease and blood to be diverted to the muscles so you can effectively fight or run. You may have noticed that when you're extremely upset, you lose your appetite and get a stomachache if you try to eat. This is because your digestive system shuts down. It's unnatural to cry and eat at the same time.

Acute stress passes fairly quickly, but sub-acute stress can last a long time. Have you ever noticed that during times of chronic, long-term stress, your body just seems to hold onto weight? You're not imagining it. The body reacts to prolonged chronic stress by storing fat. Why? Because you may need to fight or run at any moment. The saber-toothed tiger could come back! When whatever you're worried about happens and the chronic stress becomes acute, you won't be able to eat. So your body helpfully stores fat during times of sub-acute stress so you have the reserves to fight or run when you need it.

One last tip… Find an enjoyable pastime that can capture and hold your attention. I mentioned in the chapter on "The Importance of Self-Care" that people with hobbies tend to be happier in their lives. Hobbies also are a potent distraction from thinking about food, and simply thinking about food can make you hungry. It triggers the flow of digestive juices. Find something engaging to do so you're not sitting around thinking about your next meal!

PART 4

ISSUES & ANSWERS

THOUGHT STOPPING

I've mentioned thought-stopping throughout this book in many contexts, but it's such a useful technique that I want to talk about it more generally. You can use thought-stopping with any unhelpful thought you can't get out of your head – counting calories, calculating fat grams, romantic obsession, obsessive worry, negative self-talk ("I'm gross", "I can't do this"), or negative self-indoctrination ("Healthy eating means dieting and restriction").

Whenever the unhelpful or obsessive thought pops into your head, mentally say to yourself "No!" (not out loud, inside your head). And then, depending on the type of thought you're stopping, do one of two things: redirect your attention or correct the lie.

OBSESSIVE THOUGHTS

If it's an obsession (romantic obsession, obsessive worry, or any other thought going around and around inside your head), redirect your attention to the input of your five senses. What do you see? What do you hear? What does the air feel like on your skin? Touch the fabric of your clothes and notice the texture. Look at the pattern of the floor tiles or the carpet. This brings you out of your head and into present moment.

At first your mind will revert again in about five seconds to whatever you're obsessing on. That's okay. Don't get mad at yourself or chastise yourself for it. It's just the nature of obsession. Gently bring yourself back to the present moment by again saying "No!" to yourself, and redirecting your attention to the input of your five senses.

At first you may have to do this a dozen or more times an hour, but eventually your subconscious will get the message that you're not going to allow your mind to dwell there, and the obsessive thought will become less frequent. Eventually, if you are consistent, the thought will stop popping into your head. But you have to be vigilant and consistent about this. Never allow yourself to indulge in the obsessive thought, or your unconscious will continue putting the thought in your head.

Redirecting attention to your five senses also is an effective way to stop calculating the calorie, fat, or carbohydrate content of the food you eat. Many people who have spent years dieting do this automatically and find it hard to stop.

NEGATIVE THOUGHTS

How you feel about something depends entirely on how you think about it. If you speak to someone and he is inattentive and barely notices you, your feelings about this depend on how you interpret his action. If you think he's inattentive because of his personal response to you – that he can't be bothered talking to someone who's fat, for example – then you will be hurt and angry. If you learn that the man just received some terrible news, then you will not take his response to you personally and you'll feel compassion rather than anger.

What you think about something is reflected in your self-talk – the automatic thoughts that go through your head all day long. If your automatic thoughts are self-abusive ("I'm disgusting", "I can't do anything right"), then your self-esteem will be low and you'll probably be depressed. If your automatic thoughts reinforce old, irrelevant ideas ("Eating a salad means I'm dieting and can't have desserts"), then you'll stay stuck in the past and be unable to move forward.

If you're stopping a negative thought, then after saying "No!" to yourself, redirect your attention to the truth. Correct the negative thought. For example, if it's self-abusive, you might say, "I can do whatever I set my mind to" or "I'm a good person" or "Human beings make mistakes". If it's negative self-indoctrination, you might say, "Providing my body with nourishing food is self-love and self-care" or "Denying my body the nourishment it needs is self-deprivation".

These are just examples. You'll have to adjust the counter-statement to the specific situation. Don't make it a general platitude – be very specific.

Thought-stopping is a simple technique, but very powerful and effective. Try it. You'll be surprised at the difference it can make.

THE ROLE OF EXERCISE

The sooner you can break the association between exercise and weight loss, the better. When you see exercise as an aspect of dieting, you may rebel against it and not want to do it.

Exercise isn't about being slim, it's about being fit. And in fact it generally won't make you slim. The calories you burn make you hungrier so you tend to eat more. Exercise has many important health benefits, but what you eat has far greater influence on what you weigh. So when you first start exercising after you stop dieting, just keep repeating to yourself that you're doing this to be healthy, not to be slim.

Being slim and being fit are not the same. You can be slim and unfit, unable to walk up a flight of stairs without becoming winded. You also can be overweight and fit. There have been some interesting studies about this.

A moderate amount of extra fat has no negative impact on health in and of itself. It appears to harm health because being heavier is correlated with exercising less and being less fit. But actually, it's being less fit that has the negative impact. You have to be significantly overweight for weight alone, independent of fitness, to harm your health.

So move your body, no matter what you weigh. The health benefits are enormous, both emotional and physical. Exercise makes you feel more energetic and confident. If you're middle-aged, it makes you feel and look younger. It makes your movements more fluid and graceful. And it's a more effective anti-depressant than any pill.

NORMAL EXERCISE

I approach exercise in the same way I approach eating. I know my body and what makes it feel good, and I do what feels good. At the gym (when I go) I do aerobic exercise because I love how I feel afterwards. I've never liked lifting weights, so I don't. I've always been naturally strong and I have genetically poor aerobic capacity, so maybe it's body wisdom that always leads me to aerobics. That's where I'm weakest and need exercise the most.

I do exercises to strengthen and stretch my abdominal and back muscles because I get lower back pain otherwise. And I like to stretch the muscles in my legs because I use them a lot. I usually walk at least an hour a day, and I take the stairs rather than the elevator if it's four floors or less. Exercise doesn't have to mean going to the gym and laboring on stair steppers, stationary bikes, and treadmills.

TAKE A WALK!

I strongly encourage everyone take walks outside. Walk for a minimum of 15-20 minutes, and do it every day if you possibly can. There is no other action you can take that offers more benefits to your body, mind, and spirit.

Walking gives you a period of time each day that's just for you. No one is making demands on you, and you can have some peace and quiet. It gives you time to think.

The full-spectrum light of the Sun improves mood and counteracts depression, even on an overcast day. Some people are so affected by lack of sunlight that the shorter days of winter cause clinical depression (called Seasonal Affective Disorder, or SAD). This is treated with full spectrum indoor lights. Even if you don't have SAD, exposure to sunlight will improve your mood. You want to get depressed? Sit inside all day.

Also, the body manufactures Vitamin D from sunlight on skin. There's no other way to get this nutrient except through supplements. Since no naturally occurring food contains Vitamin D, it's often added to milk. But if you get outside, you'll have plenty of Vitamin D.

And then there are the spiritual benefits. Breathe; look up at the sky. Being outside gives you perspective on your life, and connects you with your spiritual side. You become aware of the universe around you, and how you are a part of it.

If health problems prevent you from talking a walk, at least sit outside for a while each day. But if you can walk, don't just sit, walk. Research has shown that the act of walking – putting one leg in front of the other and letting your arms swing in natural opposition to your legs – lowers blood pressure and reduces other signs of physical stress. It's the single most health-enhancing activity there is.

Walk as fast as you comfortably can. That increases the aerobic benefit, and aerobic exercise is a great mood enhancer.

A good time to take a walk is after lunch. If your schedule doesn't currently allow this, try to make arrangements so you can. This is an important act of self-care. You need this and you're entitled to it. Give yourself this gift.

CLOTHES & GROOMING

Is your closet filled with clothes that don't fit? Do you have full wardrobes in different sizes? Do you wear clothes that are worn, unflattering, or too tight because you don't want to shop until you lose weight? Do you hide under clothes that cover you like a tent?

THE BEAUTY OF CONFIDENCE

The way you dress yourself reflects how you feel about yourself, and how you feel about yourself has a huge impact on how others see you – much more than you probably realize. A person who feels confident will inspire confidence. A person who feels sexy will be sexy to others. And a person who feels worthless will not be treated well. Others tend to evaluate us as we evaluate ourselves.

When it comes to appearance, how you feel about yourself trumps everything else. You can be objectively good looking (normal weight, nice features) but if you feel ugly and worthless, you'll communicate this in a million nonverbal ways and others won't find you attractive. People will pick up on your low self-evaluation and figure you must be right – after all, you're in the best position to know!

If you good about yourself, you will communicate this, too. Nothing is more attractive than confidence. The actor and singer Queen Latifah is a great example of this. Technically she's overweight, but her confidence makes her attractive and you don't think about her weight.

Go Shopping

If you don't have clothes that fit well and flatter you, go shopping. Don't deny yourself decent clothes because you've gained weight and want to lose it first. Especially if your clothes are too tight, go shopping. Nothing makes you feel as fat and unattractive as clothes that are too tight.

If you're overweight you probably don't enjoy clothes shopping. You're forced to confront the size you take, it's hard to find clothes that fit, and the dressing room mirrors reflect your brightly lit self in your underwear, often from three sides. But it's worth braving all that to have clothes you feel good in.

The way you clothe and groom yourself telegraphs an assessment of your worth to yourself as well as to the world. When you take care with your appearance, you feel better about yourself. It's one of those small acts of self-care that I talk about in the chapter on "How to Love Yourself". Simply taking the action can improve your self-esteem.

Don't even think about buying clothes that are too small as a motivation to lose weight! That's utterly self-rejecting. When you lose weight, buy new clothes.

Once you have some decent clothes to wear, get rid of the rest. Go through your closets and your drawers, and try on every article of clothing you own. If it doesn't both fit and flatter you, toss it. If you've been saving a favorite article of clothing for the day it fits you again, toss that, too. Even if you lose enough weight to wear it, it will be out of style.

PERSONAL GROOMING

There are other aspects to self-presentation besides clothes. How's your hair? Too long? Unkempt? No shape? Both men and women will look better with a good haircut.

Not all women like wearing make-up, but if you're not philosophically opposed, learn how to apply it with skill. Subtly applied makeup can correct flaws and make you look a lot better, as can neat, well-shaped eyebrows.

Taste varies and my purpose here isn't to give advice on fashion or good places to shop. My purpose is to encourage you to take care with your appearance, no matter what your weight. Wear clothes that you feel good in, and devote time to your grooming. You'll look good, you'll feel better, and others will treat you better.

Raising Normal Eating Children

If you're a parent, you want to spare your children the problems you've faced if you can. So this question from a Normal Eating Support Group member has come up more than once:

> How can I teach my kids about their own hunger without it becoming an issue in their lives?

You don't need to teach children how to eat normally because they are born knowing how to do it. You just have to avoid disrupting what comes naturally.

Unfortunately, the disruption can start early. Some mothers feel that to maintain their sanity they need to feed infants on a schedule rather than on demand (when the infant is hungry). But I don't think this is a good idea for a child who is too young to speak. They get hungry, they're not being fed, they don't know why, and there is nothing they can do about it. That's pretty scary, and may cause the fear of hunger that so many emotional eaters experience.

Children don't have to learn to eat without guilt or discover what hunger feels like. They do this as naturally as they breathe, as long as their instincts aren't disrupted. They intuitively eat when hungry and stop when full. But they don't have the necessary nutritional knowledge to supplement body wisdom (see the chapter on "Stage 4: Choosing"). It's appropriate to require a child to eat a healthy meal before having something sweet. That doesn't teach that sweets are forbidden; it teaches healthy choices.

It's also appropriate, after infancy, to switch from demand feeding to regular meals. A normal eater (which all children originally are) easily adapts to regular meal times, once they're old enough to understand what that means. They intuitively adjust how much they eat to match the schedule.

This is mainly an issue of self-care for the parent. Children readily abuse the invitation to demand food at will to keep the parent constantly attending to them. That's not good for the child because it's not good for the parent. When your child is a parent herself, she needs to know that her needs are important, too! If a child is old enough to prepare her own meals, that's different. But if you're providing the food, then you have the right to create boundaries around what you will do. If you don't, the demands upon you will be limitless.

And then there is this short list of major no-nos:

- Never require a child to "clean his plate" or continue eating when he isn't hungry. If he's pushing food around the plate and you know that in half an hour he'll want you to make something else for him, then tell him that this is dinner, he eats it now, and there won't be more in half an hour. This is about who's in control – the child or the parent – not hunger.

- If the child took more than he can finish, it's okay to ask him to take less in the future so less food is wasted, but never require a child to finish what he took. Never force a child to eat when he's not hungry. Children waste food – that's an unavoidable fact. Throw the extra food in the trash, not down your child's throat (or your own throat).

- Never use food as a reward or bribe for good behavior.

- Never withhold food as punishment.

A child naturally uses food mainly to fuel the body. Don't break this association by forcing non-hunger eating, or using food as reward or punishment.

Lastly, don't talk about how you shouldn't be eating particular foods, or make a big deal about how much you eat, or talk about negative feelings you have about the size of your body. Try to model healthy attitudes towards food, eating, and body image as much as you can, because your children will imitate you.

Social Eating

People whose eating is fully normal – people with years of recovery, or no history of emotional eating – easily adapt to regular meal times. They intuitively adjust what they eat so they're hungry on schedule. But for people recovering from emotional eating, this is hard! If you have dinner plans with friends, how do you arrange to be hungry at the right time?

Social eating brings other complications, as well. It's difficult to eat mindfully with other people if you're just learning how to do this. If you're a guest in someone's home, the host may push you to eat more than you want. And what do you do if you're no longer hungry and everyone else at the table is still eating?

BEING HUNGRY ON SCHEDULE

A normal eater with dinner plans will plan to be hungry by eating a lighter-than-usual lunch. And they'll say so very explicitly: "I want to eat a light lunch because we're going to a great restaurant tonight and I want to be hungry." Because they know their bodies, they know how much to eat to be hungry at the right time. When you get to know your body better, you'll be able to do this, too. But when you're first reconnecting after years of ignoring hunger and satiation cues, this isn't so easy.

It may not occur to you to eat less at lunch so you can be hungry for dinner. That's the most unfortunate mistake because then you can't enjoy the food. I'm not saying you can't eat the food, but if you do, you won't really enjoy it and you'll end up uncomfortably full. The best solution is to order something small, push the food around on your plate, and then ask for a doggie bag. Most likely, no one will notice that you're not eating. But if someone comments, just say, "It's really good but I ate a big lunch. I'll take it home with me."

At the other extreme, you may have skipped lunch because you weren't hungry, and then feel ravenous at 5pm when you have dinner plans at 7pm. If you're at a 2 on the Hunger/Satiation Scale, you need to eat something or you'll be too hungry by dinnertime. Your instinct will be to satiate your hunger, but resist this. It's very disappointing to not be hungry for a delicious meal. Eat just a very small amount, two or three bites. This is hard to do because you'll still be hungry, but maybe a 3 rather than a 2. That will take the edge off feeling ravenous without spoiling your appetite for dinner.

MINDFUL EATING WITH OTHERS

For someone whose eating is fully normal, monitoring hunger and satiation cues is effortless. It's like what happens when you learn to drive a car. At first it's hard to pay attention to all the many things a driver must monitor, but eventually you can do it automatically and with ease. A new driver cannot carry on a conversation while driving; an experienced driver can.

It's similar with mindful eating. Over time you'll be able to stay mindfully aware of your eating while having a conversation. That said, you don't have to eat and talk at the same time!

Next time you're out for dinner with friends, watch for this common pattern. There is much conversation while waiting for the food to arrive, and then after the food is served, conversation stops almost completely for a while. Maybe someone will comment that the food is good, but for the next 5-10 minutes, people mostly eat rather than talk. That's because true hunger makes food more interesting than anything else. You want to fully focus on your eating experience so you can enjoy it.

Don't feel uncomfortable or self-conscious about focusing on your food, and using your mouth to chew rather than talk. That's the normal and natural thing to do.

STOPPING WHEN FULL

Just because others are still eating doesn't mean you have to keep eating. If you're a woman and your dinner companion is a man, matching what he eats is a good way to guarantee that you'll overeat. Women don't need as much food as men. If you're done and he's still eating, just put down your fork and continue the conversation. You don't have to be eating to sit at the table with others. Social eating is about companionship and conversation. There's no requirement that you be eating the entire time.

The stickiest problem in social eating is a host who tries to push food on you, urging you to take seconds when you've had enough, or to try a food you don't want. It is possible – really, it is – to be firmly assertive without being rude. It is perfectly all right to say, "The food is wonderful but I'm full, and I can't eat another bite." If your host doesn't accept this response, then your host is the one who's being rude. If she continues to push, she's disrespecting your boundaries.

You always have the right to take care of yourself. Other people's feelings matter, but not more than your own well-being.

TELLING OTHERS
WHAT YOU'RE DOING

If you're with a group of friends and they're all talking about their diets or how they ate something they shouldn't have, what do you do — especially if you used to participate in discussions like these? Do you tell them about Normal Eating?

What about the people you live with? Should you tell them about Normal Eating?

TELLING FRIENDS

What makes this difficult is that Normal Eating is the road less traveled. Many people believe that the only way to achieve and maintain a normal weight is through strict adherence to a diet. They're wrong. 95% of the people who lose weight on diets regain it, plus some. Normal Eating is the most reliable path to permanent weight loss. But do you want to have this argument? Do you want to be put into a position of defending yourself?

The guiding principle with friends is whether sharing what you're doing will make your path easier or harder. If they don't live with you, they don't need to know. If you think they'll be receptive and supportive, by all means tell them. If they have weight issues of their own, they may want to try Normal Eating themselves. But if you don't think they'll support you, just listen and say nothing, and be glad you're not still on the diet merry-go-round yourself. Don't create unnecessary problems for yourself.

TELLING FAMILY

You do need to tell the people you live with what you're doing, even if you can anticipate an argument. Changes in how you eat will be evident to them, and they may ask you directly why you're eating something that's "not on your diet". Also, changes in what you eat may affect what they eat, especially if you're the one who does the cooking.

Hopefully your family will be supportive; they'll embrace what you're doing and want to learn more. But if they're not, you must set clear boundaries. You cannot allow inappropriate comments and criticism to drive you into hiding what you eat. That will seriously undermine your progress.

Family members need to understand what you're doing because you live with them. They also must be very clear on the fact that even if they don't agree with what you're doing, it is your right to do it. Set the boundary: They are not allowed to comment on your weight or your eating. To do so is disrespectful and harmful to you. If they continue to make inappropriate comments, remind them in the moment, every time they do it, that this is an out-of-bounds topic. (See the chapter on "Healthy Boundaries" for more.)

THE NORMAL EATING
SUPPORT GROUP

The Normal Eating Support Group is a vibrant and active online community that was founded in 2002 and is still going strong. As of this writing the message base contains over 45,000 posts, with more than 3,600 of these from me. It's a great place to ask questions, receive support, and learn how Normal Eating has helped others.

Support is important when you're working on Normal Eating since this is the road less traveled. People can make it very hard to stay on the path to recovery. With the Normal Eating Support Group, you always have that support.

The camaraderie and acceptance you'll find in the forum also is very healing. Many people who struggle with compulsive eating and excess weight are filled with self-loathing, and feel completely alone in their struggle. It's a revelation and a relief to learn that others feel exactly as you do. Your forum friendships can help you to accept and love yourself, crucial elements of the Normal Eating process.

Normal Eating involves working through the issues you eat over, and these can be hard to uncover. Reading posts from others can help you to make connections in your own life that you might not see otherwise. There's also nothing more encouraging than seeing someone just like you succeed. You'll read many success stories in the forum.

The Normal Eating book addresses the most common questions people have, but you'll find much more in the forum message base – sleep eating and night eating, sexuality, diet soda, and much more. There's an excellent search engine for locating posts on any topic. Or if you have a question that hasn't been addressed, just ask!

You can learn a lot just by reading, but the best way to use the forum is to actively participate. Ask questions; share your struggles and successes. The people who post the most tend to make the fastest progress in Normal Eating. There is no such thing as posting too much!

THE JOY OF FREEDOM

Not everyone who is overweight is an emotional eater. Some people just need to learn better eating habits. If that's your only problem you can skip the first three stages of Normal Eating and go right to Stage 4, Choosing.

But if you're an emotional eater, you can't simply choose better eating habits, as I'm sure you know from having tried and failed. You can't choose at all until you first free yourself from the grip of compulsion. Stages 1, 2, and 3 free you from compulsion so you *can* make good eating choices.

No one likes to be fat, but the worst part of emotional eating isn't that it makes you fat. The worst part is the obsession with your weight, the compulsion around food, the unmet needs, and the self-loathing. Emotional eating puts you at war with yourself. You're in constant inner conflict about what you eat, and under constant assault from self-recrimination. You have no inner peace, and there is no pain worse than not liking yourself.

Normal Eating addresses the problems of emotional eating directly. As you move through the stages, you learn trust in yourself and true self-care. In the end you achieve much more than normal weight; your whole life improves. It takes time and effort, but the rewards are just as great. The joy in freedom from emotional eating goes way beyond the satisfaction of weight loss.

I wish you peace and good health. You can do this!

Printed in the United States
219453BV00001B/10/P

9 780963 078179